# Transform Your Nonprofit with Inbound Marketing

## How to Turn Strangers into
## Inspired Advocates

### Brooke Freedman & Taylor Corrado

# Contents

**PART THREE: CONNECT**

**Chapter 5: Connect with Your Constituents through Social Media**

Start small

Use calls-to-action to build your following

Social media policies – do you need one?

Inbound Marketing in Action: St. Baldrick's Foundation

**Chapter 6: Turn Strangers Into Supporters with Calls-to-Action**

The inbound call-to-action defined

Primary versus secondary calls-to-action

Creating calls-to-action that convert

Inbound Marketing in Action: DoSomething.org

**Chapter 7: Capture Prospective Supporter's Information with Landing Pages**

Building effective landing pages

The form has been submitted, now what?

Inbound Marketing in Action: Tony Evans' The Urban Alternative

**PART FOUR: ENGAGE**

**Chapter 8: Educate Supporters Through Email Marketing**

Effective email marketing starts with an opt-in list

Make your content relevant – segment your list

Tips for growing your email list

# Acknowledgments

Several individuals gave us their inspiration, support and help to make this book a reality.

Thank you to Brian Halligan and Dharmesh Shah for your vision for making marketing that people love and for giving us the opportunity to do the same for nonprofits.

Thank you to Beth Kanter for blazing the trail for all nonprofits, large and small, and for encouraging them to take that first step to helping others and continue to do so with every failure and success.

Thank you to our nonprofit team, who keeps us moving forward every day. Thank you to the ever positive and encouraging Dianna Huff for making this book possible.

But most of all, thank you to the organizations that contributed to our book as key examples, as well as the organizations out there working and fighting for a cause for they feel so strongly.

# Foreword

I first discovered HubSpot and the idea of "Inbound Marketing" when I noticed an online fundraiser that HubSpot co-founder Dharmesh Shah was doing in 2010 to support the nonprofit, Room to Read. He was giving away copies of his book, *Inbound Marketing: Get Found Using Google, Social Media, and Blogs*, in exchange for a donation to this important organization. I bought the book, read it, and then reached out to Dharmesh asking if I could give away a free copy on my blog.

He said yes – and more. A few months later, he sent me 40 free copies of *Inbound Marketing* to give away to nonprofits during workshops that I was facilitating based on my first book, *The Networked Nonprofit*. *Inbound Marketing* was a terrific complement to my work.

I've spent my whole professional career working in, for, and with nonprofit organizations. Most of that time has been spent helping nonprofits think about strategy as well as the mindset changes and skills required to embrace new online technologies to support their mission-driven work. As I witnessed the birth of the World Wide Web in 1992, and later social media and mobile, I saw that nonprofits faced challenges in adopting these new tools. The major challenge was the lack of time needed to acquire and internalize new skills in the face of limited resources.

When I started blogging in 2003, blogs and nonprofit social media use was in the embryonic stages and – as is usual for disruptive technology – was viewed with raised eyebrows by nonprofit leaders regarding its value. This skepticism is why I wrote *The Networked Nonprofit* with Alison Fine. I wanted to help the millions of staff people and board members of nonprofit organizations get over the fear of change and make their way into this new social world.

Aimed at nonprofit leaders, *The Networked Nonprofit* helped them take those first steps toward being successful at managing social change in an age of connectedness – pave the way for organizational adoption. The book walked nonprofit leaders through the process of transitioning their thinking and orientation from managing organizations to participating in and managing social networks. But participating is only halfway down the path to successful outcomes.

My second book, *Measuring the Networked Nonprofit*, with co-author KD Paine, takes a look at how organizations can complete the journey by using data to measure results and make improvements. But the book doesn't cover strategy and tactics, which are also important, especially for inbound marketing.

While I've known about HubSpot and inbound marketing for several years, I didn't know the inside details of HubSpot's social media history until I read the chapters-in-progress of the book you're holding. Midway through, Ellie Mirman, Head of SMB (small / mid-size business) Marketing, tells the story about HubSpot's beginnings with social media as part of its overall inbound marketing strategy. Ellie joined the company in 2007 – shortly after its founding. As one of two people on the marketing team (the other was her boss), she was charged with developing the company's marketing, which consisted of two assets: a datasheet and the beta of what is today's HubSpot Inbound Marketing software. To generate awareness, Ellie created an e-book and offered a webinar. Two small steps to be sure, but each month, Ellie – and others who were hired after her – kept producing content, trying new social media platforms, and measuring their efforts to see what worked. According to Ellie, they made mistakes. She even confesses that she didn't "get" Twitter at first and thought it was "stupid." The marketing team's consistent efforts paid off, however. Today HubSpot has tens of thousands of followers on social media. It publishes blog posts daily and offers a large variety of content offers each month. Ellie shared the lessons she learned because starting small and growing incrementally, the way HubSpot did, is a surefire way for your nonprofit to be successful, too.

**Building your (big) online presence starts with baby steps**

As a Master Trainer, I've had the joy of traveling the globe and working with nonprofits on every continent of the world (except Antarctica). My work revolves around helping nonprofits become "networked nonprofits" – or what HubSpot refers to as Inbound Nonprofits. By this, I mean nonprofits that successfully use inbound marketing tactics and internal cultures to spread their mission, design and scale programs, communicate with stakeholders, and inspire behavioral change. Inbound Nonprofits are also masters at using data to improve results. Successful Inbound Nonprofits use these tactics and tools to make the world a better place. But getting to the inbound mindset doesn't happen overnight.

I know from experience how difficult it is to make the leap into effective practice with a new technology tool. In 1992, the New York Foundation for the Arts hired me to serve as the network weaver for ArtsWire, an online network of arts organizations and

12

artists. ArtsWire enabled both artists and arts administrators to use the Internet to connect with one another – and to learn how to use online communications technologies to support their missions. I taught hundreds of workshops to thousands of arts organizations to help them establish their very first website, use email to connect with supporters, take their first foray into online fundraising, and to use search to find information online.

When I started my work, I didn't know a modem from a microwave. I wasn't a natural born techie or marketing geek. I had the passion to learn, but when I taught myself, I would often fail – resulting in hours of wasted time. What helped me was working side-by-side with a small group of Internet geeks who generously and patiently showed me all the shortcuts. They shared their tips – which helped me be more effective at helping nonprofits embrace the Internet.

In their book, *Transforming Your Nonprofit with Inbound Marketing: How to Turn Strangers into Inspired Advocates*, Taylor Corrado and Brooke Freedman, of HubSpot's nonprofit team, are those patient geeks. They explain how to implement a successful inbound marketing strategy that's based on the company's proven Inbound Marketing Methodology: Attract, Connect, Engage and

Inspire. You attract strangers – people who may not know about your organization – to your website and using various tactics, including calls-to-action and landing pages, connect those strangers with your organization through relevant content, eventually turning them into donors, fundraisers, volunteers or members, who ultimately become vocal advocates and activists for your cause.

*Transforming Your Nonprofit* is strong for two reasons. First, it gives you the "big picture" that's often lacking when it comes to marketing your nonprofit online. Sure, you know you should be using social media, email, content, etc., but how exactly does it fit into your overall marketing strategy? More important, why do you need it? Taylor and Brooke explain why. Two, this book walks you through the stages of the Inbound Marketing Methodology created by HubSpot of turning people into supporters and advocates. In its way, HubSpot's Inbound Marketing Methodology mirrors the "Crawl, Walk, Run, Fly" methodology I advocate for nonprofits. "Okay," say Taylor and Brooke, "You've optimized your website. You're writing a blog post twice a month. You have a Facebook page and people have liked it. You're growing your email list. Now let's convert some of those people with a call-to-action." Each chapter builds on the other, so that by the time you get to the end, you have a framework for attracting people to your organization and moving them along what Taylor and Brooke call the "giving cycle" – moving them to become donors, fundraisers, volunteers, members, and eventually inspired advocates.

In short, you have a framework for attaining your organization's mission that can be implemented – one step at a time. And Taylor and Brooke should know because HubSpot did it using the very framework you're holding in your hands. If they can do it starting with a datasheet, you can, too.

-- Beth Kanter, Master Trainer, Blogger and co-author, *Measuring the Networked Nonprofit* |**www.bethkanter.org** | Twitter: @KANTER

# Introduction

Building awareness for your organization's mission used to be relatively straightforward. You and your staff used the bulk of time and resources on one-to-many marketing tactics such as solicitation letters, glossy print newsletters, and in-person events. Whether you were a local or national organization, you might also use PR, radio, TV, transportation signage and other traditional methods for getting the word out about your cause.

The problem, however, is that while these tactics still work in some cases – according to research by the Stanford Social Innovation Review, survey results show that while 70 percent of respondents agree that they learn about a cause through traditional media – they're quickly becoming less effective for a number of reasons. One, individuals have become harder to reach; two, research shows that people – especially Millennials (the 25 – 34 age group) – get involved with causes in ways that traditional nonprofit methodologies ignore; and three, social media has completely shifted how your donors, volunteers, members, and fundraisers now interact with your organization.

**People are harder to reach**

At the 2012 HubSpot INBOUND marketing conference, Brian Halligan, HubSpot's co-founder and CEO talked about his life differs from his dad's life.

"My dad had three inputs into his life: he watched TV, he read two newspapers a day, and he talked on the phone a lot – especially at work. If you wanted to reach my dad by phone, you dialed 411 and asked Information for either his work or home number. My dad came home from work every day at 6:30 and would sit at the kitchen table opening his mail. He got a lot of mail, and he read everything, so this would take about twenty minutes. My dad also read the *Boston Globe* newspaper everyday. He – and his friends, co-workers, and neighbors – all watched the same television shows and sat through the same commercials night after night (this was of course before DVRs and remotes). If you wanted to reach my father, it was easy: call him, advertise to him through traditional media or send him mail.

"My life is very different from my father's," Brian went on. "I hate the telephone. I hate the phone so much I don't answer many calls (except from my investors – ha!) and use Caller ID to screen who is calling. At HubSpot, I don't have an office. I have a desk. The only time I open mail is when I put my MacBook Air on my desk and it starts to slide off due to the mountain of mail sitting there. That's when I open my mail. I don't read the print newspaper. I pay bills online. Email – that used to be a good way to reach me, but I use Gmail, and Gmail comes with this nifty Priority Inbox feature. I tell Gmail which messages I want to see at the top of my inbox – the rest get filtered below the priority messages. Guess which ones I respond to?"

While Brian is talking about the changes that have affected how consumers shop, learn and live, these very same rapid changes have affected nonprofits as well. As new technological mediums have disrupted old ones, we've adapted habits in response – almost without thinking about it. For example, consider how we accessed breaking news only ten years ago and technology, such as Twitter, has changed these habits.

**The "fundraising pyramid" has changed**

The top of your fundraising pyramid is just that – a small, concentrated piece of your whole universe, made up of older, rich donors who, though important, won't be able to add to the strong foundation of your future fundraising efforts. While they're reliable for contributing large sums of money to help you reach your yearly goal, they are high risk, high reward from an investment of time and resources perspective. Inbound Nonprofits have learned the secret of inverting the pyramid; instead of focusing on the few rich donors at the top (as seen in Figure 1), they've shifted their focus to the people who comprise the pyramid's "base" and "core" – their recurring and annual donors.

## The Fundraising Pyramid

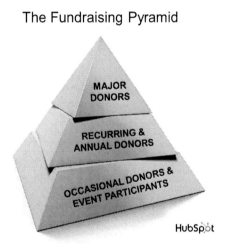

*Figure 1: The Fundraising Pyramid*

Why the change? These groups consist of the Millennial (20-35) and Gen-X (36-50) generations – the very people riding (and even driving) the wave after wave of technological innovation. If you focus on building the relationships with these individuals, sharing stories they can relate to and providing the information they're looking for, they'll naturally down the inverted pyramid, and over their lifetime they'll become the major, rich donors that you know so well. As you'll read in later chapters, Gen X and Millennials are fluent when it comes to technology and how to use it, from shopping and paying bills to connecting with friends, families and the organizations they care about.

**Your donors are now in control**

Despite our seemingly disconnected world, and the moats we've built around ourselves, our need to connect is stronger than ever. This need for connection extends to the causes and people we care about – whether it's purchasing and consuming "local" organic food or supporting critically ill family members through fundraising events. According to Blackbaud's 2011 Peer-to-Peer Event Fundraising Consumer Survey, 69 percent of respondents reported they take action because of their affinity to a cause – with an organization's mission and impact being its greatest differentiators. "Peer-to-peer fundraising is personal," state the authors of the survey. "Organizations can support this personal activity by coaching participants to share their story."

As a nonprofit executive or marketer, your job, which has always been challenging, is now even more so. You face myriad challenges – from a "greying" of your donor base to banging your head trying to figure out how to reach seemingly unreachable people. To successfully reach and engage your target constituents, *you must now match the way you build awareness about your organization and its mission with how your donors, volunteers, fundraisers and members want to connect with you.* That's what you'll learn with this book. Whether you're a fledging organization or an established one, you'll learn how to use inbound marketing tactics to grow your nonprofit and turn strangers into supporters, fundraisers and new donors – people who eventually become inspired advocates for your cause.

**Inbound Marketing is a new way to connect with your audience**

Where did the term "inbound marketing" come from? Our founders, Brian Halligan and Dharmesh Shah, came up with this term to describe the process Dharmesh was using to get his blog, OnStartups.com, "found" by thousands of people online. Started in 2005 as part of his thesis work at MIT, Dharmesh's blog pulled in more interest and more traffic than most of the venture-backed startups Brian was working with before founding HubSpot. When Brian and Dharmesh began talking, they used the term "outbound" to describe traditional marketing practices, such as tradeshows, direct mail, and telemarketing (practices that were becoming less effective as Brian was quickly learning at his job), and "inbound" to describe what Dharmesh was doing – writing blog posts and commenting on others, posting his content to social media sites, etc. HubSpot, which they founded in 2006, was born out of those conversations. (You can read their full story in their book, *Inbound Marketing: Get Found using Google, Social Media, and Blogs*, Wiley 2010.)

The principle concept of inbound marketing, which we'll cover in detail in Chapter 1, is about creating a new system of reaching your constituents. Over the years HubSpot has mastered inbound marketing practices through its work with almost 10,000 businesses and enterprises, including several hundred nonprofits (as of 2013). But, like Brian and Dharmesh, we, too, kept seeing a sea of change with regard to nonprofits and how they generated awareness. Due in part to lower start-up costs, these organizations used the new tools, such as websites and blogs, social media, and email marketing, to promote their causes and generate awareness far beyond their local borders. Inbound marketing is what separated these new organizations from more established nonprofits.

**Why we wrote this book**

The nonprofit organizations we work with fall into two groups: they either understand the value of inbound marketing but get confused by the "business" language surrounding it (leads, conversions, cost per lead, etc.). If you're working at one of these nonprofits, this book will give you a new vocabulary specific to nonprofits to help give clarity to what HubSpot has been preaching to businesses, as well as compelling information that you can use to help "sell" inbound to your board members or management team. The second type of nonprofit organizations we work with are those who know they need to change their marketing and fundraising mindset but don't know how to get started. If you can relate to this, then this book is for you!

This book will take you step-by-step through the stages of the Inbound Marketing Methodology for Nonprofits. You'll learn insights into what each stage means as well as discover best practices and marketing tools you should use to support your inbound marketing strategy. To spark your creativity, you'll find real world examples and case studies throughout the book that show how other Inbound Nonprofits have been successful.

We hope you find this book helpful – and we thank you in advance for reading it. Without you and your organizations, we couldn't do what we love – helping organizations maximize their awareness for causes that change lives around the world. To be even a small part of something bigger makes everything we do that much more fulfilling. If you like what you read, or you have questions, you can find us personally on Twitter or LinkedIn – or the nonprofit section of the HubSpot blog. Please do connect with us – we'd love to hear your stories and how we can help in any way!

Taylor Corrado, Marketing Manager, Nonprofits & Higher Education

Brooke Freedman, Sales Manager, Nonprofits & Higher Education

August 2013

# Part One

# Inbound Marketing for Nonprofits

*"Turn strangers into friends. Turn friends into donors. And then... do the most important job: Turn your donors into fundraisers."*
**Flipping the Funnel -Seth Godin**

# Chapter 1
# The Inbound Marketing Methodology

Over the past five years, marketers have witnessed a tectonic shift in strategy, from campaign-based interruption marketing, to a consistently measured, closed-loop inbound marketing strategy – one that pulls interested donors to your organization and creates lasting relationships. Successful inbound organizations have recognized that success depends on shifting their focus from interruption-based marketing toward a more donor-focused strategy; in fact, 50 percent of respondents to the *2013 State of Inbound Marketing Report* indicated they consider their organizations as primarily customer or donor focused.

As a holistic, data-driven strategy, inbound marketing involves attracting and converting visitors into donors through personalized, relevant information and content and following them through the four distinct stages of the Inbound Marketing

Methodology illustrated in Figure 1.

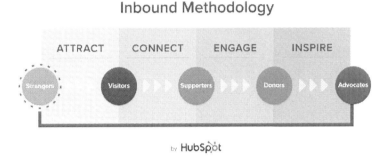

Figure 1: The Inbound Marketing Methodology for Nonprofits

**Attract, Connect, Engage, Inspire**

More than the latest buzzword, inbound marketing has

traction. According to our research, nearly 60 percent of marketers

at all types of organizations around the world have adopted inbound

marketing strategies and more than 80 percent of those executing

inbound marketing have integrated it into broader organizational

goals. Organizational budgets, too, have reflected this change, with

marketing costs having grown 50 percent from 2010 to 2013. (*2013

State of Inbound Marketing Report*).

Inbound marketing isn't about creating content and "pushing

it out" into the world, hoping the right people will see it. Instead, it involves an ideology and framework for attracting and connecting website visitors with your mission, so they become those valuable, committed constituents, with personalized, relevant information and content. It's about meeting people at the right time at every stage of their research and decision making process using a cohesive methodology. As a result of years of hands-on use and testing, we've synthesized inbound marketing into a holistic, data-driven nonprofit specific methodology comprised of four stages, Attract, Connect, Engage, and Inspire. It's this proven Methodology upon which this book is based.

**Attract – Get the right people to your website**

The first stage of the Inbound Marketing Methodology, "Attract" is the process of driving traffic to your website – traffic that's comprised of "strangers" or people you don't know who have an interest in your organization or mission, want to potentially donate to or solicit funds on your behalf, and ultimately become advocates for your cause. But, how do you find these people? More importantly, how do they find you?

The first step is to know whom you want to attract. In traditional outbound marketing speak, this is called your "demographic." A demographic is historically defined by the age, gender, job title, zip code and household income of an organization's target audience. With inbound marketing and new analytical tools, we can now define our ideal constituent groups through the use of "personas."

Personas, which are much more comprehensive than demographics, incorporate what your constituents are really like, inside and out. Personas encompass the lifestyles, goals, challenges, and aspirations of your constituents – as well as personal and demographic information. Creating personas is a very important first step in re-defining your organization as an inbound nonprofit because the process helps you begin to see things from your constituents' perspective versus your own. You'll learn how to develop your own personas in Chapter 2.

Once you have your personas in place, you can then create the content that attracts them to your website. Some of the most important tools for attracting your ideal personas include search engine optimization (SEO), blogging, and social media. You'll learn about each tactic in chapters 3, 4 and 5 respectively.

**Connect – Educate your visitors into prospective supporters**

In the second stage of the Inbound Marketing Methodology, you provide your website visitors with educational information, whether through videos, photos, blog articles, how-to guides or annual reports, about your organization to connect them to your mission or cause. You want these individuals to find something of value or to learn more about your organization – information that only you can provide, whether it's personal stories about your constituents, volunteers, individuals impacted by your efforts or an annual report showing the proof of your previous years of work. Content is the key to gaining the trust of these visitors so that eventually they provide you with their contact information, whether by downloading content, signing up for an e-newsletter, or subscribing to your blog. By providing you with their email address and opting into your contact list, you're then able to engage these individuals into the next stage of the Methodology through email marketing and nurturing.

To offer this type of content and capture valuable contact information, inbound nonprofits use contextual calls-to-action and landing pages. You'll learn about each of these tactics in Chapters 6 and 7.

**Engage – Turn supporters into donors / fundraisers / volunteers**

Once you've attracted the right people and have captured their contact information, you're then ready to transform them into committed, engaged constituents. In this third stage of the Inbound Marketing Methodology, you'll connect with your prospects and drive them to take action through email marketing and nurturing – sending the right content to the right people at the right time. To do so, you must first build and segment your email list by your personas: donors, fundraiser, members, volunteers, sponsors and even your staff. You'll learn about how to grow and segment your contact list in Chapter 8.

Now comes the really fun part of the Inbound Marketing Methodology – lead nurturing. By lead nurturing, we mean moving prospects through the giving cycle using email marketing automation. By moving them through the giving cycle's three stages – awareness, evaluation, and action – and sending content appropriate to each persona and stage, you're able to more effectively turn prospects into engaged constituents. You'll learn how to put lead nurturing to work in Chapter 9.

**Inspire – Allow people to spread awareness on your behalf**

The wonderful part of inbound marketing is reaching the fourth stage of the Inbound Marketing Methodology – Inspiring people to become advocates for your organization. Advocates, in effect, become part of your marketing and fundraising or development department because they spread your mission and tell stories about working or supporting your organization with their friends, family, co-workers and networks to become involved with your organization, too. This ultimately draws in a new network of personally connected individuals who will turn into engaged constituents. You'll learn more about inspiring your constituents in chapter 10.

**Storytelling with content helps build trust**

Content is the glue that holds inbound marketing together – and it has many benefits. Content answers the questions your ideal constituents have about your organization, your cause, your efforts, and your impact – whether it's within your local community or the world. By answering people's questions with content, you build trust and motivate people to want to connect with you. But, the content developed by your organization isn't just about answering the "what." It also answers the "how" and "why."

This is where storytelling plays a critical role with regard to a nonprofit's content strategy: One, storytelling highlights the achievements of both your organization and your constituents; and two, it shows proof of your organization's impact. In fact, storytelling has become such a crucial component of fundraising that several sessions were devoted to it at the 2013 Nonprofit Technology Conference. Reports Michael DeLong at the TechSoup.org blog, "Four years ago, nonprofits and libraries were just picking up on the power of digital stories. Now they are considered an indispensable part of your organization's marketing and fundraising strategy."[1] Storytelling can be done through your website or a blog, social media, and email marketing with photos, videos and actual written stories. The more channels through which you share your stories, the more likely they are to be seen and shared by your intended audience.

In June of 2013, for example, charity: water went to the field to shoot video footage for the launch of their 2013 September Campaign. As they worked, they also took pictures of the people in India already impacted by their partner's work of providing clean water and shared these photos and brief stories on Instagram (see Figures 2 – 4).

---

[1] http://forums.techsoup.org/cs/community/b/tsblog/archive/2013/04/23/digital-storytelling-at-the-nonprofit-technology-conference-2013.aspx

*Figures 2 – 4: charity: water used Instagram to share stories of women positively impacted by the organization's partner, GramVikas', work in India.*

While the content itself is beautiful and inspiring, the stories about each woman play an important role: they help connect charity: water's supporters and their contribution to the persons being positively impacted. The mission of charity: water is more than simply providing clean water – it's also about changing the lives of women such as those portrayed in the photos. By sharing the women's stories, charity: water shows its contributors this impact – and in the process, inspires their constituents to share these stories with their networks, thus attracting more people to the organization.

When people show your content some love in the form of sharing it commenting on it, etc., it helps build your organization's social proof (which we discuss in Chapter 5), as well as extend your reach. By "reach," we mean that instead of promoting your content to just your existing base, your supporters and advocates share it with their networks – which gives you far more exposure, or reach, than you could ever hope to get on your own. Imagine you have 100 people tweeting, sharing and talking about your organization and each person has 250 people in their network – you now have the potential of 25,000 people learning about your cause. And because our networks are made up of mostly of individuals we're personally connected to, when we share information that's important to us, our friends, family members, and colleagues are more likely to want to read and share it, too. That's the power of contextual and lovable content.

**Inbound Marketing in Action: charity: water**

With over 34,000 Likes, 1.3 million Twitter followers and 141,000 G+ fans (as of this writing), charity: water is using the Inbound Marketing Methodology to reach prospective donors, volunteers, advocates and employees. The organization, whose mission is to bring safe and clean drinking water to developing nations, regularly tweets and posts about their work in the field – posts which get retweeted and shared across the social web – and in doing so, has significantly advanced its outreach since its founding in 2006. In 2012, for example, the Bill and Melinda Gates Foundation listed the organization as one of its top five most impactful charities for holiday giving in a 2012 blog post by Meghan Casserly of Forbes. Also in 2012, charity: water received a Google Global Impact Award and was asked by the New York Stock Exchange to ring the closing bell.

What's charity: water's secret? After the founder, Scott Harrison, spent two years on a volunteer mission in Libya, he let advocates take control. Instead of relying on the traditional methods to attract and move donors up the "fundraising pyramid," Scott wanted to empower his supporters and encourage them to create their own fundraising campaigns through charity: water's in-house peer-to-peer platform.

"It all happened organically," says Paull Young, Director of Digital. "In 2006, Scott threw a party to celebrate his 31st birthday and the launch of charity: water. He charged $20 at the door and sent all the funds he collected to a refugee camp in northern Uganda; the organization used 100 percent of the funds to build three new wells and fix three broken wells. Scott sent pictures and the GPS coordinates to everyone he knew. A year later he said,

'Let's do it bigger.'" charity: water contacted people with September birthdays and asked if they would ask their friends, families, co-workers etc., for donations that matched their ages versus gifts. By 2008 the organization was crowdfunding and using social media to get the word out. The response was overwhelming and as a result, the organization built mycharitywater.org in 2009 (Figure 5).

*Figure 5: mycharity:water.org fundraising platform*

The website, which Paull refers to as a "fundraising platform," allows people to set up their own fundraising campaigns. Once they click on charity: water's "Get Involved" tab, potential fundraisers are walked through four steps for setting up their own campaign and getting their personal networks to donate.

To showcase how others have done it, charity: water uses real people and their creative ideas, such as giving up your birthday or wedding gifts, running a marathon and even sky diving! "We let people do whatever they want," says Paull. "We're aware of the ways people are raising money, but we don't control the process or them. People are using our platform to do amazing things."

Showing social proof using online media is one of the pillars of charity: water's success. Fundraisers create their own videos and photos showing how they help the clean water crisis, which they share with their networks and which charity: water shares with is its own network of supporters, companies and celebrities – a double cycle that increases outreach while encouraging and inspiring still more people to get involved. Passionate advocates for charity: water are as young as age five, with one nine year old creating a design for a t-shirt, asking for donations instead of trying to make a profit, and raising $5,000.

"In the nearly four years since we launched my.charitywater.org, we've raised over $25 million from over 25,000 fundraisers of all types - not just birthdays. We're working out where to take it next," says Paull. "Our goal is $100 million in 2015 with 80% coming from digital. Our fundraising platform is the core of our business. We're using it to reinvent charity" – and in the process, empower their constituents to help take the organization to the next level. Imagine what your donors could achieve if they were in charge.

**To Do:**

1. List all the ways you attract people to your website. Pick two that need the most improvement and focus on those.

2. Look at your website through the Inbound Marketing Methodology. What are you doing to Attract, Convert, Engage, and Inspire your constituents? What areas do you want to focus on and why?

3. Look at a website of a nonprofit with whom you're engaged. What compelled you to connect – and what keeps you connected?

4. _____

5. _____

(We'll leave a few extra blank in each chapter for you to list other "to-do's" that come to mind.)

# Chapter 2
# **Creating Donor Personas**

Before we dive into the first stage of the Inbound Marketing
Methodology, we need to discuss how to identify whom you're
targeting when you begin implementing the new marketing
strategies outlined in this book. The individuals you're trying to
attract, connect, engage and inspire are your organization's
personas. Fictional representations of your ideal constituents,
personas are a customized profile that describe the various goals
and observed behavior patterns among your organization's different
constituents groups. Personas are based on real data, including
demographics and known behaviors, as well as data gathered by
surveys or interviews, about your constituents' personal histories,
inspirations and concerns.

Developing personas helps you segment and target your constituents more effectively and allows you to provide them with the right content and information they seek to connect them to your cause or mission – and eventually become advocates for it. According to Tommy Landry, Founder and President of Return on Now, personas are particularly important now that Google is ranking websites in the post-Panda/Penguin world with regard to relevance. "Panda incorporates metrics that indicate **how readers respond to the content** (bounce rate, time on page/site, page views/visit, etc.," he writes on his Return on Now blog.[2] When people respond to relevant content, Google rewards the website or page with higher search engine rankings over time. (We talk more about search engine optimization in Chapter 3). By incorporating personas into your marketing, your organization takes the first step toward becoming a donor-centered Inbound Nonprofit. You also begin the process of creating marketing that's very targeted and focused toward your specific donor-base. Targeted, focused content, as you'll learn with this book, is what drive return on investment.

When developing your personas, you break down your target audience into broadly drawn, fictional characters by

---

[2] http://returnonnow.com/2011/07/seo-content-strategy-importance-personas/

constituent types: donors, members, volunteers, fundraisers, sponsors, corporate partners, etc. (You may even break these down further, such as new versus recurring donors). Each persona is given specific traits based on what they're trying to achieve and their behavior patterns inside and outside of their interactions with your organization. Combined together, these traits make up your personas and will help guide you as you work to serve and reach them with inbound marketing.

In this chapter, you'll learn why it's important to develop personas and what you need to do to get started.

**Getting started with your personas**

You create personas through research, surveys and interviews of your entire constituent base – both "veteran" and new. By going directly "to the source," you're able to collect data that's both qualitative and quantitative, and in turn, you're able to paint clear pictures of your ideal constituents, what inspires them, why and how they become connected to causes. Once your interviews are complete and you have your research in hand, you'll then identify patterns in order to segment your constituents by persona type. When this step is done, you'll then name your personas and give each one a "face" by finding a photo that best illustrates who this person is or someone who looks similar to those you interviewed.

It helps if you break your constituent types into groups and then sub-groups. For example, if your organization's cause is medical related, you might have the following constituent groups and sub-groups so you can better target your audiences with contextual content:

| Donors | Fundraisers | Volunteers |
|---|---|---|
| Individuals | People in the community | Friends or family of affected people |
| Local businesses | Local businesses | Local businesses |
| Existing donors | Friends or family of affected people | Members |

You should refer back to each person group at the start of any fundraising campaign or event.

**Get to know your constituents**

To get as much meaty data as possible, it helps if you can interview at least three to five people for each type of constituent you have (i.e. donors, fundraisers, volunteers, etc.). Make a list of potential people to interview; to get accurate data, reach out to those who have been connected to your organization for a while as well as those who've just come on board. If possible, include people who used to be connected with you but aren't any longer – you'll want to learn what causes people to "disconnect" or become uninterested in your cause. Also consider "influencers" – those who are quite vocal on social networks about your cause but haven't become involved or donated.

To increase the likelihood of people willing to be interviewed by you, offer something in return. A simple Amazon or iTunes gift card is an easy way to encourage people to take the time to be interviewed. Or, if they're deeply involved in your organization, a free t-shirt or free registration to your next event would be a great incentive. When recruiting interviewees, it also pays to be very clear that you will not be soliciting for donations during the call or the in-person interview. Be clear that you're doing research and that you want to learn from them in order to provide deeper experiences with your organization for them and future constituents.

**Ask questions specific to behaviors**

You want to ask questions that will help you get to know your constituents better so that you can understand what motivates them – and then create content and experiences that engage them. The types of questions you should ask depend on your particular organization. You can tailor questions to your specific cause; for example, if your organization rescues cats, you could ask, "How many rescued cats do you have?" or "Have you fostered a cat?" If your organization offers fundraising events, you could ask your interviewees why they became involved (e.g. because of an affected family member or friend or because it's an endurance event, and they like to compete). Additional questions include: What is your job role and title? Where did you go to school and what did you study? Describe your career path. How did you end up where you are today? Do you use social media? If yes, which platforms? Which organizations do you follow on social media? Which publications or blogs do you read? Of which associations are you a member?

Some people aren't good at expressing themselves or reflecting on their own behaviors, so be sure to ask "why?' as a follow up. If someone says to you, "I'm not on any social networks!" don't simply move on to the next question. Stop and ask, "Why is that?" If the person says, "Because I feel uncomfortable on them," again ask, "Why?" Keep asking "why?" until you get at the core of a person's behavior or driver. As you're interviewing, listen carefully for "sound bites" that sum up the person. For example, Sally, a college student, may not donate a lot of money but in her interview she says, "I like to inspire others to support missions that are close to their heart." This is a perfect time to ask, "Why?" You might learn that Sally may be one of you best advocates and influencers or she may give you a great marketing or fundraising idea.

Listen carefully for objections or concerns. Your interviewees may tell you they can't find an easy way to give to an organization online. Or they may want to see where their donations are going and the impact they're having before they commit to a cause. These are pieces of qualitative information you can use to compile your personas. And finally, while you're listening, jot down any buzzwords your interviewees use and note their mannerisms. Did he or she use lots of colloquial expressions, such as "Awesome!" or was the person educated and refined in speech? Was the person reserved or excited and chatty?

To gather basic demographic and personal data, you can survey your constituents through online surveys prior to the interviews. We advise that you keep these surveys brief (no more than five questions) and that you allow people to remain anonymous.

**Create your personas**

Once you've gone through the interview process, you'll have lots of meaty raw data about your potential, current, and past constituents. But how do you distill this data so that it's easy for everyone to understand? As you go through the data, look for patterns among the different interviewees and then roughly group these patterns into potential personas. To keep things simple, first develop one persona that you can share with your team. (You can input your data for a donor persona into our template we've created:

**http://offers.hubspot.com/donor-persona-template**). After your team agrees on this one persona, you can then create any other personas you need. Give each of your personas a name that makes sense, such as Volunteer Vicky or Member Mike. Adding a face to your persona helps you envision what he or she looks like. You can visit sites such as istockphoto.com or Creative Commons on Flickr and search for images that exemplify what your persona might look like based on your demographic data. Add this photograph to your persona template (see Figure 1).

# Sample Sally

**BACKGROUND:**
- Student at Boston University
- Volunteers for Red Cross
- Studying Political Science and President of her sorority.

**DEMOGRAPHICS:**
- Female
- Age 18-25
- Dual HH Income: less than $25,000
- Urban

**IDENTIFIERS:**
- Enthusiastic personality
- Social media savvy
- Follows several organizations on Twitter and Facebook. Subscribed to several volunteer blogs.

*Figure 1: An example of a donor persona with picture.*

Once you have completed this process, you should have detailed descriptions of your personas' demographics, needs and behaviors. The more detail you pack into your persona profiles, the easier it will be to create content for each of your target groups – as well as knowing where to promote it. You'll also know how to create content for your website based on personas – which we'll discuss in the next chapter. Lastly, make sure to share your developed personas with each staff member. Include them in your training materials and presentations. The only way for personas to work effectively is if everyone in your organization knows them inside and out, and refers to them on a weekly, if not daily basis.

**To Do:**

1. Download the HubSpot Donor Persona Template:

   **http://offers.hubspot.com/donor-persona-template**

2. Follow the step-by-step process for developing personas.

3. Intermediate: If you've already developed your personas, start thinking about the specific content types that would appeal to each persona. Map your content or editorial calendar to your personas.

4. _____

5. _____

# Part Two

# **Attract**

*"If you find yourself in a hole, the first thing to do is stop digging."*
**- Guy Kawasaki**

# Chapter 3
# Attract Visitors to Your Site with SEO

The fundamental piece of Stage One of the Inbound Marketing Methodology is search engine optimization, or SEO, which is the art and science of ensuring your website and associated content (landing pages, blogs, etc.) *gets found* in search engines, such as Google or Bing, by individuals who are searching for related topic or keyword phrases.

SEO is divided into two types: on-page SEO and off-page SEO. On-page SEO, which includes keywords, meta tags, URLs and page headers, comprises about twenty-five percent[3] of the overall impact your SEO efforts will have in how your site ranks for any particular search phrase. (By "rank," we mean where on the

---

[3] *Learning SEO from the Experts: How to Master Every Aspect of Search Engine Optimization for Business Success*, HubSpot e-book, Curated by Anum Hussain

search results page your website is listed – top, middle, bottom –

and on which page – first page, second page, third page, etc.) The

remaining seventy-five percent is due to off-page tactics, including

building authority, trust and credibility with contextual content

through inbound link building, blogging, co-marketing, social media

and public relations (PR). In this chapter you'll learn the basics of

both on-page and off-page SEO. We'll also briefly cover Google Plus

and Pay-Per-Click (PPC) and how they can impact your SEO.

**On-page SEO: Optimizing your website for crawlers and visitors**

On-page SEO refers to the process of optimizing your site

content so that it's clear to crawlers and to visitors what each page is

about. The goal is to have any given page of your website be

aligned – from top to bottom – around a specific topic or call-to-

action. By this we mean everything, from title and meta tags to the

URL and headers, all refer to a specific keyword or keywords.

Keywords play an important role in search, because, when

you perform an online search, you use phrases – or keywords – you

believe will deliver the most relevant information you're looking for. If

the search engine doesn't return what you're looking for, you refine

your search using different search phrases until you get what you

need. Keywords, then, are the heart of SEO (both on-page and off-page). Selecting the right ones for your own optimization strategy is very important because you want your content to be *optimized for and to relate to the keywords visitors are using in their searches.* Doing so helps ensure the right visitors find your website's content. Think back to your personas – what keywords would they be searching for to get them to find your website? Be sure to optimize your website's content with those keywords.

Choosing the right keywords is relatively simple – you simply use a keyword search tool. These tools, which take the guesswork out of keyword research, show you the number of searches for a specific time period per keyword/search phrase. What if one of your keywords has zero searches? Say "hurray!" Now you know **not** to use this keyword in your optimization efforts as it means few of your constituents are using it in their searches. A number of SEO tools exist that have a keyword tool built in – you can try moz.com's SEO toolbar found at **http://moz.com/tools/seo-toolbar**. HubSpot's software also includes a keyword search tool.

Choosing the right keywords is important for another reason as well: Google and Bing use crawlers (or automated programs) to find new pages to add to their indexes. These crawlers use the keywords on your pages in order to know when to display them to searchers: "Is this page about cancer awareness? Yes. Great! Let's show it." The three most important places to use keywords are: meta tags, specifically title and description, URLs and page headers, and the title of the page's content, such as a blog post title or headline.

**Meta tags**

Meta tags are the official data tags located in the HTML source code for each page of your website. Because they're located in the source code, people don't see them on your page content, although they do appear in your browser tab. For SEO purposes, you want to focus on two specific meta tags: the title tag and the meta description tag. When the search engine crawlers come to your website, they use these two tags (and other various components) to determine what your page is about and for which searches it should rank.

Title tags, which should contain no more than 100 characters, describe the contents of the associated webpage. Title tags are the first aspect of your page that a search engine comes across when crawling your website. Google and Bing use title tags to determine relevancy and ranking, so they're very important to your SEO strategy. Each page of your site needs to have its own unique title tag. For example, your "About Us" page would have a different title tag than your "How to Give," page. The more specific the title tag, the more relevant your web pages will be to related searches, resulting in a higher ranking. The biggest SEO mistake people make is to use generic words in the title tag, such as, "Home," "About," "Community", or just your organization's name on each page. None of your potential constituents would use these phrases to look for an organization like yours!

Figure 1: A visual representation of a Title tag on redcross.org/support

Meta description tags, which should be no more than 160 characters, also describe the content of a website's page. While search engines don't use meta descriptions to determine ranking position, searchers often use them to determine the relevancy of your information. To help searchers determine the relevancy of your content, it's a good practice to include your keywords and the main call-to-action in your meta description tag. As with title tags, each page of your site should have its own unique meta description tag.

While you don't see a page's title and meta description tags when you view the content of a webpage, you do see the title tag in the browser tab and you see the title and meta description tags in the search results. Figure 2 shows charity: water's HTML source code for its homepage. We've underlined the title and meta description tags.

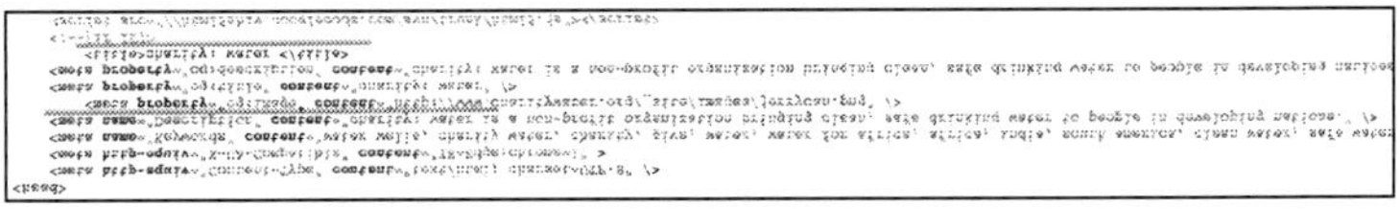

*Figure 2: charity: water's HTML source code showing meta information*

Now let's look at how the search engines use these tags. In Figure 3, you can see charity: water's Google listing – which is what you see if you search "charity water." The blue hyperlink is the title tag. The "snippet" of information is the meta description tag.

*Figure 3: charity: water's Google listing*

## URLs

Another powerful signal a page can send to search engines is its unique identifier or URL. URLs are used to guide both search engines and visitors to relevant content. However, not all URLs are created equal. In the following example, the bad URL includes the nonprofit's name, but the file name, "xyzbz3," is gobbledygook. You have no idea what the page is about.

**Bad URL**: www.nonprofitname.org/xyzbz3

**Optimized URL:** www.nonprofitname.org/cancer-walk-2013

The optimized URL, on the other hand, lets crawlers and visitors know what the page is about through the use of well-selected keywords – "cancer-walk-2013." Most content management systems (CMS) include simple editors that allow you to create "visitor friendly" URLs like this.

Google and Bing display a page's URL, along with the

hyperlink and snippet, in the search results, so using a keyword or keyword phrase to describe what's on the page helps searchers to determine if your content is relevant. One important thing to note: The keywords closest to the forward slash are the most important for SEO, so keep them as close to the forward slash as possible when creating new URLs.

**Page headers**

Page headers are simply the bolded headlines and sub-headers you see on web pages and blogs that provide the visual and contextual clues about the content. Page headers allow readers to quickly skim content in order to find the information they value (or can safely skip). Search engines give more weight to header text than to the body content on your page. Therefore, it's important to use keyword-optimized headers that have been properly tagged.

Header tags look like this in the HTML source code: <H1>, <H2>, <H3>, etc. Google and Bing give more weight to H1 tags than to H2 tags and more weight to H2 tags than to H3 tags. So it pays to include your keywords in H1 and H2 tags. For example, a nonprofit might use the following headers:

**H1** (main header text): Cancer Walk 2013

**H2** (secondary headers, less SEO weight):

- Tenth Annual Cancer Walk

- Cancer Walk 2013 Beneficiaries

- Cancer Walk 2013 Registration Information

## Off-Page SEO: Building authority, trust, and a reputation

Off-page SEO was long defined by the quantity, quality and relevance of links to an organization's website – links that established SEO authority and that influenced search results ranking. An organization could build its authority and reputation by getting sites to link to it; the more links a site had, the more its authority and reputation grew. The problem, however, was that authority and reputation was defined only by number of links, disregarding relevancy, and because of this, too many organizations (and companies) used nefarious tactics to "scam" the search engine algorithm in order to have their websites ranked higher. Today, a website's authority and reputation are built through the types of conversations people have about an organization and the references made about them by other websites through link building, blogging, co-marketing, social media and PR.

## SEO and link building (aka *link earning*)

Search engine algorithms rank websites, pages and blog posts on numerous factors, including the quantity and quality of links that point to said website or page. The more trustworthy your website or page appears to be (e.g. the more high-quality sites linking to it), the higher it will rank in the search engine results. For example, the *New York Times* linking to your website will give you more SEO authority than a no name blogger. The old way to build links included tactics such as article marketing (where you wrote an article and then rearranged the words to transform the article into multiple versions), paying for links in directories, and other low-quality "spammy" tactics that are now penalized by Google.

Link building today focuses on *earning* links. Organizations do this by creating high-quality, original contextual content that provides value to visitors as well as engages them. This content can come in many forms, such as a nonprofit's blog, e-books or white papers, video, and podcasts (to name just a few). When individuals find value in this content, they'll often share it – either on social networks or their own websites or blogs. This sharing is what creates links back to a website – and is what helps build even higher authority and trust from search engines. Most importantly, keep a balance between quality and quantity. While a large number of links is helpful, the quality of those links is equally as important.

**SEO and blogging**

Blogging is a terrific way to create unique, contextual content that others will want to share, link to, and comment on. For every new blog post, a new page is created and indexed by search engines. The more pages indexed, the more opportunities available for your constituents to find your website. We'll discuss blogging in greater detail in Chapter 5.

**SEO and co-marketing**

Co-marketing defines the efforts of cross promoting, networking and community building. It's a partnership between two or more organizations, or your organization and a like-minded company, in which each participant promotes the other's content, services, or mission / cause.  The United Way, and its partnerships with corporations and the National Football League, is a good example of co-marketing. When organizations agree to co-market or partner, they give each other access to some of their "internal" information, whether it's email lists or social networks. By co-marketing, each organization increases its respective reach, which in turn increases the likelihood of shares and inbound links.

**SEO and social media**

Search engines are now incorporating social content into their search results. Do a search for an organization, for example, and you'll often see listings for that nonprofit's Facebook, Twitter, LinkedIn, Google Plus and YouTube profiles. Google+ even shows which of your friends liked these pages. This factoring in of social media is referred to as "social search." In social search, content that has a connection to the searcher is prioritized. For example, if you do a search for an organization, Google and Bing might display a search results page that includes tweets or Facebook postings from people in your network about that organization. Alternately, some forms of social search prioritize content that has been shared by social media influencers, even if these experts aren't directly tied to you.

Google and Bing display these social search results based on authority and relevance: if someone in your network has liked a smartphone app for a nonprofit's Facebook page, for example, and you do a search for an app, that page your friend has liked has a good chance of appearing in your search results. Since you know this person, you're more inclined to trust his or her expertise or recommendation. As a nonprofit, you can use social search to help build the authority of and people's trust in your organization. It's also another way to attract new constituents through your existing base's social networks with SEO (an inbound marketing trifecta!).

**SEO and public relations**

Traditionally, organizations have used press releases to get the word out about new initiatives, events, or even partnerships and sponsors. When released through online wire services, such as PRWeb.com, press releases have important off-page SEO benefits as well. Each time you distribute a release via a wire service, you create a new link. When syndication websites pick up these releases, more links get created. Even better, bloggers, journalists and industry publications pick up your release and either reprint it word-for-word or write an article in their own publication or blog about your news – which creates valuable inbound links, not to mention trust, authority and credibility.

One trick to maximizing the value of optimized press releases is to create content that others would want to share, such as an annual report or original industry research reports. To improve your results, promote genuine and ethical dialogue-driven content with bloggers, influencers and social media leaders. The better your relationships are with these influential people, the more willing they are to write about your organization and share your news.

**Give your content a boost with Google+**

While people debate whether Google+ users will overtake Facebook, one thing we're positive about is that if your organization doesn't have a Google+ presence, you're missing out on a great way to boost traffic and improve your search engine rankings. Google's Facebook-like social network, Google+ is gaining traction as Google adds more features to it – making it an essential tool for all kinds of organizations. For nonprofits operating on limited budgets, using Google+ actively is like putting your social SEO on steroids – you get maximum return with relatively little effort. This is because *Google includes G+ profiles, pages and posts in its search engine results pages* – often above other content. Content that others have "+1" (very similar to Facebook's "Like" button) gets displayed higher in the search results than content that isn't tied to Google's network.

In addition, Google Authorship is playing a bigger role with regard to building authority, reputation and credibility. If you've noticed people's pictures next to content in the search results, then you're seeing Google Authorship at play. With this feature enabled,

70

bloggers, authors – and yes, even your executive director – can tell Google and the world that they've authored an original piece of content. In Figure 3, for example, you can see people's pictures next to the content they've authored. Authorship also offers a key SEO benefit as research is proving that it significantly improves click-through rates from the search engine results pages – by up to 150 percent according to some data.

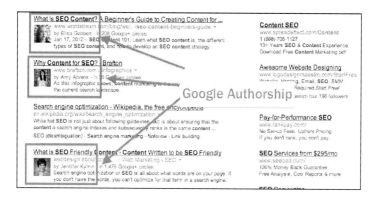

Figure 3: Example of a search page showing Google Authorship

**SEO and Pay-Per-Click**

Both Google and Bing allow companies to purchase advertising on their search engines. Also known as "Pay-Per-Click," these ads are the "sponsored" listings you see at the top and right side of most search engine results pages. What many nonprofits don't know about, or haven't taken advantage of, is a special program called Google Grants (**see www.google.com/nonprofits**).

With this program, nonprofits can apply for a $10K in-kind grant that

can be used for free Pay-Per-Click advertising (on Google, of

course). Google awards one grant every month.

With Google Grants, you can build awareness about your

organization, capture email addresses through landing pages, and

gain Facebook Likes and Twitter followers. It's one of the most

under-utilized tools out there – and a huge missed opportunity for

nonprofits. We encourage you to learn more about Google Grants by

visiting the Google Grants page. If you're one of the lucky nonprofits

to receive a grant, be sure to view our webinar presentation on how

to set up your Google Adwords account:

**http://offers.hubspot.com/google-grants-webinar.**

**Inbound Marketing in Action: Open Doors**

Founded in 1955, Open Doors is a fundraising and relief

organization that helps Christians worldwide persecuted for their

religious beliefs. When oppressive governments ban other

organizations or force them out of the country, Open Doors assists

those in need and helps to strengthen affected communities.

Building awareness was Open Doors' main goal as it's this

awareness that drives donations, which in turn help more people. For many years, the organization's marketing efforts were mainly driven by direct mail, but they knew they needed to change to an online, inbound strategy.

Building an online presence, which included a new website and growing their Facebook and Twitter followings, was the first step in the organization's inbound strategy. However, while Open Doors did successfully increase traffic to their website through SEO and social media, the marketing team didn't know how people were learning about them, nor did they have a system for capturing people's contact information. In addition, they needed a better way to encourage their constituents to make donations. To achieve their goals, the team signed up for HubSpot's inbound marketing software.

Using HubSpot, the team was able to embed forms into their website pages, an action that enabled them to capture information about their new website visitors and then follow up. Using email, versus direct mail, the organization lowered their marketing costs while driving more donations – and increase traffic back to their site by 348% the first year.

**To Do:**

1. Use our Marketer Grader tool to see where you can improve your website's SEO: **http://marketing.grader.com**.

2. Complete a website audit of all your Title tags. Make each page's Title tag unique to the information on the page.

3._____

4._____

5. _____

# Chapter 4
# **Attract New Visitors to Your Website by Blogging**

"In today's environment where communication is much more streamlined," says Derrick Feldman, CEO of Achieve and co-author of *Cause for a Change: The Why and How of Nonprofit Millennial Engagement*. "Nonprofits need to help people understand that by 'clicking this' they'll get something in the end. We have to help people understand that if they read something and participate, they're helping contribute to an end goal." As Derrick succinctly states, content is what helps you connect with your audience on a personal level and encourages them to support your organization by spreading your mission within their own network of friends, family, and colleagues. Inbound nonprofits use various forms of content to spread awareness of their cause, attract new constituents, and re-engage past supporters.

One of the most effective methods for creating and sharing content on a regular basis is by blogging. A blog, which should be part of your organization's website, is a place where you can post content "on the fly" as news or events happen, engage visitors through inspiring stories, and have a dialogue with your readers and constituents. A blog also makes it very easy (from a technology standpoint) to incorporate images, pictures, audio or video that powerfully communicate stories that touch people's emotions and personally connects them to your cause. Contrast a blog with sharing your stories the traditional way – through a print newsletter or direct mail that has to be mailed and is then subsequently sent to the recycle bin. Expensive and time consuming – and definitely not share-worthy! Blog content, in contrast, is personal, relevant, and online forever.

Blogging has many benefits. One, it's the single most effective way to increase your organization's credibility online as it enables you to share your stories and be the thought-leader for your cause. Two, blogging helps you rank higher in the search engines for keywords or phrases related to your organization. Three, a blog simplifies your marketing strategy. And four, a blog gives you valuable real estate in which to place calls-to-action for offers that help connect strangers with your organization through your website. In this chapter, we'll look at each benefit in detail and then share a few ways you can create blog content.

## A blog increases your organization's credibility online

As we discussed in Chapter One, we've all built "moats" around ourselves. It's harder to reach us by phone, direct mail or traditional advertising. Due to the vast changes in how we communicate with each other and how we source our news and information, the onus is now on organizations to "prove" their credibility to prospective constituents through what Feldman calls "tangible transparency." "Tangible transparency," says Feldman, "is clearly articulating what is the action you want people to take and what will happen if the person takes it. For example, if you donate $10, this will happen. If you spread this message, this is how you contribute to the end goal. Tangible actions of people can move us from one end of spectrum to the other in order to accomplish goals."

By sharing your stories, and showing the impact of your constituents' support of your cause, you help potential constituents deeply understand the problem your organization helps solve and how their actions – large or small – contribute to the mission. By showing the results of your organization's impact, you build trust and credibility through what's called "social proof."

Social proof, according to Wikipedia, "is a psychological phenomenon where people assume [or take on] the actions of others in an attempt to reflect correct behavior for a given situation."[4] In other words, our family, peers, co-workers and friends influence us. For example, let's say your friend reads one of charity: water's blog posts. Because she's so inspired by the thousands of people who have pledged their birthdays, she's decided to support the organization and give up her next birthday as well. She then posts an "ask" to everyone in her Facebook network to give $27 to the organization through her fundraising page on her 27th birthday rather than buying her a gift. You see her post and decide to support the organization by donating on her birthday pledge page – and contemplate pledging your birthday as well. The personal connection draws you into supporting the organization that you may not have found on your own.

Social proof comes into play two ways: because your friend is a supporter of charity: water's mission, you're now more receptive

[4] http://en.wikipedia.org/wiki/Social_proof

to their message simply because of your friend's support ("If she's supporting this organization, I guess it must be good," you think). And, when you visit the organization's blog, you're influenced by the social proof that's "tangibly transparent" in the form of stories shared, the number of dollars raised, the wells built, the number of birthday pledges, the Tweets by followers, etc.

A blog, then, helps you build trust and credibility. When your constituents share your blog posts with their networks, they help you increase your organization's awareness. They may also comment on your blog posts, an action that allows you to interact with them and get to know why they support your cause, or to simply see if your content is resonating with your blog audience. When visitors come to your blog and see your stories, results and comments from those in your community, they're positively influenced to want to connect with your organization, because others have already done so.

**Blogging helps you rank higher in the search engines**

An optimized blog filled with relevant content helps your organization get found by individuals searching for cause-related information. charity: water, for example, writes about topics relating to clean water, including sanitation, water pollution and hygiene. People searching for information on these topics will ultimately find information about charity: water. If they stumble upon the organization's blog, they may be inspired to give or fundraise.

By blogging, you can attract new visitors and then familiarize them with your organization after they've found the information they were searching for. How is a blog different from the rest of your website? Unlike the main sections of your website, which aren't updated regularly, a blog is dynamic: content is created on a daily or weekly basis and people leave comments, link to it and share it. Due to RSS (Really Simple Syndication), search engines index blog posts fairly quickly – sometimes within an hour of being posted. Hence, a blog is a great way to get relevant, timely content into the search engines on a consistent basis.

Within the SEO framework, optimizing your posts is essential to helping searchers find them. As with your static webpages, you can optimize a blog post's title and meta description tags, its URL and the post title and headlines. And, how often you blog matters with regard to ranking and getting found. Our research has shown that organizations that blog have 55 percent more website visitors and 434 percent more indexed pages! Organizations that blog 16 – 20 times a month double their traffic versus those that blog fewer than four times a month because of all the new content being indexed – and found by searchers.

In addition to helping you increase relevant traffic (that is, the people visiting your site want to know more about your cause), a blog also helps significantly with inbound link building – by up to 97 percent more, according to our research. As you create relevant posts that tell your stories, other bloggers link to your posts. Journalists, too, find blogs useful and will either read them before contacting organizations for interview requests or will link to them in their stories. And, if your content is really remarkable, it can get "syndicated," meaning an industry portal picks up your blog feed and displays your posts, along with other organizations' blogs, further extending your reach and building important links.

## A blog simplifies your marketing program

When we talk to nonprofits about blogging, they worry about adding work and complexity. For a small team already stretched thin, adding a blog – and its associated content creation– can feel overwhelming and a bit daunting. A blog, however, simplifies your marketing as it accomplishes multiple goals with a single thoughtful stream of content. With a blog, you can manage search engine optimization (which we've already discussed), reaching out to constituents through comments and feedback, public relations, and brand building and also recruiting.

**A blog gives you a place for contextual calls-to-action buttons**

Once you get visitors to your blog, you'll want to retain them by engaging them further with your website and other content. You do this through well placed calls-to-action. We call these "contextual calls-to-action" or CTAs. When you create your CTAs, you want to match the content you've written to the offer you want to highlight. For example, if your blog post is about an upcoming event and you want people to volunteer for it, you could create a hyperlink or call-to-action button within the post saying, "Volunteer for This Event!" or, "Learn About Volunteer Opportunities," which then links to a page that describes the event, the types of volunteer jobs needed to be filled, and a form people can fill out in order to sign up.

When you make your CTAs contextual, you create a seamless connection between the post and the call-to-action, as well as cater to the reader who is ready to learn more about the topic. A contextual call-to-action is much more appealing and has a much higher click-through rate than a non-contextual CTA. You have three places on your blog in which to place CTAs: the blog sidebar, within blog posts, and in post footers. We discuss calls-to-action in detail in Chapter Six.

## A blog helps with public relations

Having a blog eliminates writing arduous, multi-page pitches for news organizations. Instead of writing pitches (that probably get deleted anyway), you can create blog posts that tell the story of your organization's impact, spotlight your organizational milestones or announce new events. Once these posts are written, you can then send a quick email, with a link to the post, to your contacts at news organizations. Which would you rather read, a self-serving pitch or a warm, friendly and educational blog post that has a great picture or video attached? Your news contacts feel the same way.

## A blog reinforces your brand

Great nonprofit brands are built through storytelling and by communicating your organization's values and vision. Because you're sharing stories on your blog, you're consistently reinforcing your organization's values, priorities, mission, and cause. Building your organization's brand also helps with recruiting volunteers, members, fundraisers, donors and even prospective employees. A blog allows you to fully communicate what your organization stands for far more than a static and corporate-y "About Us" page can. A blog puts a face (or many faces) to your organization and gives your team a voice.

**How to create blog content**

Finding topics to blog about is one of the most common challenges nonprofits face. In this section, you'll find six ways to create content for your blog, from spotlighting constituents to creating evergreen content.. But first, let's address the burning question everyone asks us. "How often should we blog?" The answer, according to Josh Hallett, Director of Voce Connect, is, "You blog as often as you want people to pay attention to you." Basically, this means that if you want your constituents' attention on a regular basis – and we're thinking you want it more than once or twice a month – then you'll want to blog at least twice a week to get started, if not more.

To easily manage what you'll post about and when, it helps to create an editorial calendar. Using this calendar, whether it's physical or online, you'll be able to map your blogging frequency and schedule, filling in each blog "date" with a topic. Mapping out your editorial calendar also helps you maintain a healthy balance between content types: sharing stories, event announcements and updates, event reporting, constituent spotlights, and news about your organization's impact, to name a few things. Plan for blog content to be published at certain designated times, but also allow space to take advantage of breaking news and current events that tie back to your cause. HubSpot uses a company-shared Google Doc (that's free!) to manage who is writing blog content on a monthly basis.

As we write this, the news and social media is filled with stories about the bombings at the Boston Marathon in April 2013. National and local nonprofits are communicating through blogs; the American Red Cross, for example ran a post (Figure 1) late race day from Gaby Skovia, stationed in Afghanistan, about what it was like for him to witness the bombings – both as a service personnel and as a runner. The post includes information for people looking for loved ones. The blog sidebar includes a call-to-action to donate. When breaking news happens that affects your organization and/or your constituents, you want to publish as fast as possible – no matter what's slated on your editorial calendar. (Writing posts based on breaking news is commonly referred to as "newsjacking.")

*Figure 1: Blog post written the same day as the Boston Marathon bombings.*

Now that we've covered the basics, what should you blog about? Of course, it depends on your nonprofit and your mission and cause, but in general, keep these ideas in mind: Reach out to constituents, tell personal stories, tie donor actions to numbers and results, highlight constituents and their work, and develop evergreen content that you can use over and over again.

### Tip #1: Reach out to constituents

When you write a blog post, you can ask your readers for their input into your topic. Asking people to comment creates dialogue – between you and your constituents and between them and their peers. A blog is a great place to discuss issues, share success stories, and garner feedback. Yes, sometimes you may get some negative feedback – which is actually good. When this happens, you have the opportunity to fix something and in the process, make your constituents love you even more.

**Tip #2: Tell and share personal stories**

The most powerful blog posts connect the reader emotionally to the story being told – especially when they're told via video. Charity: water created a touching and inspiring video of 9-year old Rachel Beckwith, a fundraiser who was tragically killed in a car accident before she reached her fundraising goal. Her story sparked thousands of individuals across the world to donate to her fundraising page in her honor -- raising over $1.2 million. The video (as of this writing) has over 61,000 views on YouTube and continues to inspire individuals to give years after Rachel started her initial campaign.

You don't have to use video to tell all of your stories. A touching and heartfelt post illustrated with photos works just as well. St. Baldrick's Foundation, an organization whose mission is to fund childhood cancer grants, lets parents of cancer patients share their stories on the organization's blog. In one post (Figure 2), Lori Miller, mom to Justin Miller, writes poignantly about what it's like to send her son into the lead-lined treatment where he "feels like a caged animal," as well as her hope for his recovery and survival – even as he's been diagnosed with cancer for the sixth time.

*Figure 2: An example of a post that tells a story courtesy of St. Balderick's Foundation*

### Tip #3: Tie donor actions to numbers

Explaining how a donation directly impacts your organization's mission is sometimes made easier with numbers. You can tie the donation amount to singular units the way Nothing but Nets does. When someone donates $10, for example, the organization is able to purchase a mosquito net for one child living in a country where malaria and other blood-borne diseases are rampant. Or, you can show the overall impact of your organization's fundraisers. In another blog post, St. Baldrick's posted a photo of the Quinnipiac University Ice Hockey Team in Hamden, Connecticut. The team raised $25,000 for cancer research by shaving their heads.

Showing the impact of constituents' support is key to getting people to come back and give again. The more concrete you can make the impact, the easier it is for people to see their impact and give again – as well as share your organization's mission or cause with their personal networks.

**Tip #4: Thank constituents for their volunteer efforts**

If your organization has ways that people can volunteer their time, such as sitting on or chairing a committee, being a board member or helping out at events, you can use blog posts to highlight their efforts and to thank them for their time. (This tip is a little different from sharing people's stories about their fundraising campaigns or why they're advocates for your cause). By spotlighting your constituents and what they've done to help your organization, you get a triple benefit. One, you're thanking people for their time and effort – which always goes far; two, you inspire others to become involved (remember: social proof – we're influenced by what we see others doing); and three, when you spotlight people, they naturally tell their friends, family and co-workers through social media and email, which drives even more people back to your blog and spreads awareness instantly.

It's pretty easy to create posts that thank your constituents. Take pictures at events, give a shout-out in a post-event write-up, or let your constituents tell the world why they're involved with your organization through an interview.

**Tip #5: Repurpose evergreen content**

You know the frequently asked questions you hear repeatedly – these are the questions to which you probably already have stock answers. In addition to (or instead of) creating an FAQ page for your website, create blog posts that answer some of these questions, such as, "How can I be a successful fundraiser?" or, "Who should I email my fundraising page to, and how often should I do so?" Or, create a post that explains terms used in your industry or develop a post that lists other resources, bloggers or experts. This type of evergreen content is relatively easy to create and lasts forever – and if it's optimized, searchers will find it when looking for information over and over again.

## Tip #6: Recruit guest bloggers or hire someone to write for you

By now you may be thinking, "Wow, all of this sounds like a lot of work! We're a pretty small team." One way to alleviate the pressure of having to write blog content is to recruit people to help you. You can hire a freelancer or intern to "ghostwrite" your blog for you. This person creates content under your organization's name, freeing you up to focus on other activities. You can also divide up blog writing duties between your staff – perhaps assigning one article a month per person, or create team or department quotas.

In addition, you can recruit guest bloggers – your constituents, experts in the community, board members, or volunteers. Having guest bloggers is a win-win: You get your constituents' personal stories and fresh blog content (without having to write it all yourself); your guest bloggers get to relate why they're connected to your cause or how your organization is helping them battle cancer, save an animal's life, retrain for a job, etc. As an added bonus, when a guest blogger writes a post, you can bet he or she will share it with his or her network, increasing your organization's reach and building your credibility.

To ask people to become guest bloggers, you can put out a call on your blog and social media, or you can also ask people individually – or both! Either way, people will be flattered that you've asked. Before putting out the call, it pays to develop "author's guidelines" that explain what people can write about, how long posts should be (give people a word count range, such as 500 words), and any type of formatting you'd like them to follow. To see how one organization uses guest bloggers, we've highlighted Heartwaves, a HubSpot customer and successful blogger.

**Inbound Marketing in Action: Heartwaves Recruits 30 Bloggers, Builds Credibility**

Jared Broussard, the father of a child with a congenital heart defect (CHD), founded Heartwaves.org in early 2012 as a place for everything related to CHD and the field of Pediatric Cardiology. Designed and built for families affected by CHD, Jared wanted a platform where people could connect with each other, share information, and explore resources from other hospitals and nonprofits. Jared's goal was to be the hub of support and information for families as they embark on the challenging journey of parenting a child with a congenital heart defect.

Because he is a CHD parent himself – his son underwent complex heart surgery at the age of three months – Jared knew the kind of content he need to create. "While waiting through the anxious time our son was in surgery, I had a hope that I could use my marketing expertise to make a difference in the CHD community. The idea that became Heartwaves was literally envisioned in the waiting room – at 2:43 AM to be exact." Jared knew that his target audience would be someone like himself – a parent looking for resources stripped of medical-jargon, content developed by families for families.

Heartwaves.org initially started as a private network for patients; the network consisted of private login pages. "The system was clunky and difficult, and did not allow us to make any changes or additions to the content of the site," says Jared. Alongside the private network of personal pages, Jared launched an informational blog with posts and whitepapers using HubSpot. Initially, Jared did everything himself, including writing blog posts and whitepapers on how to prepare for your child's first surgery or how to deal with an unexpected diagnosis.

Due to the blog – and the fact that Jared was optimizing his posts and sharing them on Twitter and Facebook – his still-very-young organization began reaching thousands of people. As more people learned about the organization, Jared knew he needed to get help. "Most marketers or entrepreneurs discover rather quickly that having a vision is the easiest part of starting a business or venture," he says. "The bigger challenge is carrying out this vision with the appropriate platforms, resources and people."

Jared turned to his community and enlisted the aid of 30 people – from parents of children with CHD and adult survivors of CHD to medical experts, including pediatric cardiothoracic surgeons, pediatric cardiologists, researches and nurses. The site's credibility soared – both in terms of an improved search engine presence and with the CHD community seeing Heartwaves as a credible resource and community hub.

"The beautiful thing about Heartwaves is the passionate community," sums up Jared. "This passion has led to content that is not only credible, but also sincere, and people have responded to it."

**To Do:**

1. Create a blog if you don't have one already.

2. If you're already blogging (good for you!), double your frequency.

3. Download our blog editorial calendar template:

**http://offers.hubspot.com/blog-editorial-calendar.**

4. Intermediate: Recruit several guest bloggers to contribute on a monthly or quarterly basis.

5. _____

# Part Three

# **Connect**

*"What happens when you define a win as getting closer to someone who wants the same thing? Or when you define it as improvement over time? Or in creating trust?"*
**- Seth Godin**

# Chapter 5
# Connect with Your Constituents Through Social Media

Using social media to connect directly with constituents and build relationships – versus using it as a way to promote and push out your marketing – is what ultimately leads to increased earnings, says Jay Frost, Partner of the agency Jerold Panas, Linzy & Partners, and CEO of Fundraisinginfo.com. In a 2013 HubSpot Webinar, "More Than Marketing – Major Gifts and Social Media."

"You see it all the time. People will talk about an organization on Twitter or Facebook and 99% of the time, the organization doesn't respond," he stated. "How do you think this makes the person feel? Neglected! *This neglect is what leads to loss of donors – and revenues.* Inbound organizations know that social media is more than sending out automated messages. They use social media to thank their donors – over and over and over again – and in doing so, retain and even grow their earnings."

In this chapter, we'll show you how you can use social media to connect with your constituents using "bite-sized" manageable steps. We'll briefly cover the secondary platforms, including Instagram, Pinterest, and LinkedIn, as well as how to get started with the two primary networks, Facebook and Twitter. We'll also cover whether or not your organization needs a social media policy.

**Your constituents want to connect with you**

Whether you're using it or not, social media is integrated into all aspects of our lives: we catch up with family and friends on Facebook, witness breaking news on Twitter, tell others about the products we love on Pinterest, and share and tell stories with our photos through Instagram. While you may feel comfortable using Facebook or Twitter for your own personal use, you may feel less than comfortable when it comes to using it for your organization. For many of the nonprofits we speak with, social media is where they struggle the most. It seems easy enough to get started; what happens, however, is that organizations see little in the way of results and then and give up. This is a mistake. A huge mistake.

100

Why? Because your constituents are on these networks, interacting with other organizations, and are looking to connect with you!

In the 2012 eNonprofit Benchmarks Study, data showed that between 2010 and 2011, the media growth rate for nonprofit Facebook fan pages was an "astounding 70 percent," with nonprofits averaging 103 Facebook fans and 29 Twitter followers for every 1,000 email subscribers. If you have an email list of 100,000 individuals, that's a little over 10,000 Facebook fans and 2,900 Twitter followers. Now, think about the reach of those individuals – *the potential number of followers from your followers is exponential.* For many nonprofits, Facebook and Twitter have revolutionized the way they interact with their constituents – and indeed, raise funds, acquire members and volunteers, and build trust and credibility.

To overcome the obstacles – and fear – that some nonprofits face, we recommend that your organization start small and stay focused.

**Incorporating social media: Start with small incremental steps**

It's hard to believe, but HubSpot also started small. When Ellie Mirman, Head of SMB Marketing, started with HubSpot in 2007, she was the company's second marketer to be hired (the first was her boss, today's CMO Mike Volpe). She also had two calls-to-action with which to build her marketing empire: the beta of what is today's HubSpot software and a datasheet. From these humble beginnings, Ellie and her growing marketing team added tactics one piece at a time.

Starting small is also the advice Beth Kanter gives to nonprofits. Named one of the most influential women in technology by *Fast Company*, Beth is the co-author of *Measuring the Networked Nonprofit*. In the book, she and her co-author, KD Paine, introduce a framework called "Crawl, Walk, Run, Fly," a model designed to help nonprofits figure out what incremental steps they need to take to get to the next level. In a guest post she wrote for the HubSpot blog, "Why Every Nonprofit Should Adopt a Social Networking Mindset," Beth states, "Success can happen for nonprofits if they take small, incremental, and strategic steps." According to Beth, it's important to note that it takes months, if not years, to reach the highest level of networked nonprofit practice. "Not every nonprofit will go through the levels at the same pace," she says on her on blog, "due to organizational culture, capacity or communication objectives, program design, and target audiences."

We recommend you begin your social media efforts by building traction on one platform – either Facebook or Twitter since they have the largest user bases. By focusing on one platform, you eliminate many obstacles, including getting overwhelmed trying to learn and manage multiple platforms and trying to create custom content for each one.

Which platform is right for your organization? It depends on your goal. Do you want to build community around your cause? If yes, then Facebook is perfect for your organization. Or do you want to grow your network or reach the networks of your existing donors? If you answered yes to this question, then you'll want to start with Twitter. If you want to do both, pick one or the other and build your following and traction; once you've figured it out and things are running smoothly, then begin building your presence on the other platform. If you can't decide, survey your constituents about which platforms they're on and use the results to determine which you should invest time in first.

**Facebook: Where people connect with family and friends**

Facebook is where individuals stay connected to friends and family members. It's also a place for nonprofits to build a community of people personally connected to their cause and to spread their message through these personal channels. While you see lots of Facebook Pages with tens of thousands of "Likes, you don't need this many fans to see real results when starting out. Even a few hundred Page Likes can help you build traction: as you post content and your fans share it and comment on it, these actions appear in the newsfeeds of their friends, increasing your reach and drawing in more new people. Facebook has a few other benefits as well. You can start a private Facebook group where you can facilitate discussion around a topic and encourage your constituents to share stories with one another. You can also use Facebook to post event notices, which appear in your Fans' newsfeeds. If they check they're attending, this action appears in their friends' newsfeeds.

**The key to Facebook: Be engaging and visual**

The number one rule for successfully growing Page Likes is to always reply to people when they post on your organization's timeline or comment on one of your posts. Acknowledge people by name, and if their profiles allow it, "tag" them in your reply by using the "@" symbol – this way, your reply shows up in their notification feed. When people Like your organization's Facebook Page, take a look at their profile (if it's not private) and learn a little more about them. When you post a status update or piece of content, ask people for their feedback, insight or stories – and then thank them for sharing.

Facebook is a very visual medium and as such, images and videos get shared and liked more than other post type. You can post photos or video from events, your office or place of work (especially engaging if your work takes place in the field or at a project site). If it's ok with your constituents, post images or video of them being advocates for your cause – and share their stories. Even better, invite your constituents to share their stories and photos on your Facebook Page (you can configure your Facebook Page settings to allow people to post their own content). You can ask constituents to write blog posts (which we covered in Chapter Four) and then publicize these posts on Facebook. Your constituents will then share the content they've created with their networks – which helps increase your network and reach of your organization – leading to more Page Likes. You can also create visual infographics showing the financial impact of your organization (e.g. dollars raised). Most important though, say, "Thank you, thank you, thank you," repeatedly.

What time should you post your updates? It depends on your audience type. The best thing to do is to test. Post updates at various times of the day for a month or so to see when you get the most Likes, comments, shares, etc. And, don't forget to test days of the week including weekends. You can also use Facebook's Insights to help determine the best posting time for your organization.

**Twitter: The place to get and share news**

If you have lots of content to share – and want to grow your network – then Twitter may make sense for your organization. Compared to Facebook, sharing content on Twitter seems like much less of a commitment because the content is shorter in length and has as shorter lifetime in other people's feeds. With Twitter people retweet (RT) content they like, and in doing so, post that message to their networks via their Twitter feed, and hopefully spread the word even further.

*Figure 1: The Retweet button*

According to the Pew Research Center's Project for

Excellence in Journalism, 39% of Twitter users said most of the news they got on Twitter was material they wouldn't have read elsewhere. As a nonprofit, you can have influential people from your organization, such as a highly visible donor, supporter, spokesperson or your Executive Director, report straight from volunteer sites or other events. Sharing updates like these allow your constituents to feel connected with to an actual event even if it's happening halfway around the world.

Although Twitter isn't as visual as Facebook, you can include links to photos and video using either Twitter's Twitpic or Vine tools, or post photos using the photo-sharing app Instagram.

**Engage one-to-one or with many**

When people mention your organization on Twitter, respond! Twitter can be used as a one-to-one communication tool as well as one-to-many. When you ignore people on Twitter, the effect is the same as if you went up to introduce yourself to someone at a party, and that person simply turned and walked away. Ouch! Because people may sometimes spell your organization's name incorrectly, or not call it out using the "@" symbol, use Twitter's search function and hash tags to make sure you don't miss their posts. You can search for common misspellings of your organization's name, for example, using the Twitter search function.

As with Facebook, Twitter is also a good place to thank constituents for their work or contributions and to share their stories – again, by sharing their blog posts, retweeting their tweets, etc. We recommend you find your 10 major donors, follow them, and then thank them throughout the year. Keep them up-to-date on the progress of your organization's fundraising and engage them consistently – you'll find that they'll in turn share your updates with their (potentially wealthy) networks.

**Use calls-to-action to build your following**

Once you've determined whether Facebook or Twitter best suits your goals, you can then set up your company's Facebook Page or Twitter profile (or improve the one you already have). Because the platforms make changes on a continual basis, we won't cover specific how-to's, as the information would be outdated by the time you read it. Instead, we encourage you to visit HubSpot's Social Media Marketing Hub where you can find a plethora of resources on using social media, including basic, intermediate, and advanced how-to e-books. (Visit: hubspot.com/social-media-marketing-hub)

The key to building your following is to let your constituents know they can follow you. Add social media icons to each page of your website that links to either your Facebook Page or Twitter profile or both. (Don't worry about having "only" one icon – that's ok. Remember, "bite-sized."). If you hold live events or give online webinars, then tell people how to follow you.

To encourage people to share your content, add social share buttons to each blog post and in your e-newsletter and nurturing emails so that people can share with one click. Many email service providers and blog-hosting sites will automatically include these buttons for you.

While asking your constituents to follow you is good, you also want to make an effort and connect with or follow them. You can search for constituents on Facebook but may not be able to connect with them as many people keep their profiles private. If you have corporate donors, however, be sure your Page is a fan of their Page. For Twitter, you can find your constituents through the "Who to Follow" function. To grow your network, follow your followers' followers and browse their lists. When your constituents follow your organization on Twitter, follow them back.

**Show the love – Reward people for engaging with you**

To effectively engage your fans and followers, you need to talk *with* them, versus *at* them. While we advocate using automated tools such as Hootsuite (or the social media tools built into the HubSpot platform) to push out consistent messaging to your various audiences, relying on these at the expense of connecting with people personally and in "real time" is a common mistake. When constituents take the time to reach out to you on social media and volunteer, or raise money – reward them – by publicly responding to them and thanking them for their efforts  (if public acknowledgement is ok with them).

In addition, you want to ask constituents to participate. When you post a status update or story, ask people for their feedback. Says Jay Frost, "What you're really saying, when you don't ask for people's participation, is that you don't want to hear their voice."

**Moving beyond Facebook and Twitter**

Once you've built traction on either Facebook or Twitter, you may want to consider branching out to LinkedIn, Google+, Instagram or Pinterest. Known as the professional networking platform, LinkedIn's focus is on connecting with people you've worked with or know through a business relationship, maintaining your professional profile (which consists of your résumé) or company profile, and networking with people you know through status updates and LinkedIn Group interactions. LinkedIn is a great place to connect with major donors, corporate sponsors, volunteers, and donors through a more business-like relationship – versus the more casual and friendly networks of Facebook and Twitter.

Launched in 2011, Google+ is the second largest social platform in the world, having surpassed Twitter in January 2013 (according to Wikipedia). In addition to having SEO benefits (which we covered in Chapter Three), Google+ includes a number of pretty cool tools that nonprofits can use, including "Hangouts," a video-based chat room where you can do share screens and automatically connect to your Google Docs (perfect for teaching people how to do things online or to discuss a project), as well as a photo editing tool that lets you add cool effects to your Google+ profile cover image. Even better, because Google+ is now integrated with Gmail, once constituents indicate they're attending your Google+ event, Google will automatically add it to the users' Google calendar and then send a reminder email to their Gmail account. How's that for easy?

Launched in October 2010, and bought by Facebook in 2012, Instagram is an "online photo-sharing and social networking service that enables its users to take pictures, apply digital filters to them, and share them on a variety of social networking services, such as Facebook or Twitter" (Wikipedia) as well as through email and on Flickr. If your nonprofit uses lots of visual images to tell your story or show social proof of your mission, Instagram may make sense for you – plus it's easily incorporated with Facebook or Twitter, making it easy to share media.

Like Instagram, Pinterest is another visual platform. Launched in March 2010, Pinterest is a "pinboard-style photo-sharing website that allows users to create and manage theme-based image collections such as events, interests, and hobbies. Users can browse other pinboards for images, 're-pin' images to their own pinboards, or 'like' photos" (Wikipedia). Because it's similar to an online catalog (and has a demographic that skews heavily toward woman), data is showing that people go to Pinterest with a "shopping" mentality rather than to "engage." While some nonprofits do use it quite successfully, you should determine if it's right for your organization – and if it isn't, don't worry about it!

**Social media policies – Do you need one?**

One of the fears that many organizations harbor is that an employee will share sensitive information, disparage the organization – or worse, a donor – or spend a great deal of time on Facebook or Twitter under the guise of "working." Another issue nonprofits must address, according to Jay Frost, is whether a nonprofit's employees can personally "friend" or connect with a constituent. "Once that connection is made outside of the organization, it then brings up the question, 'Who owns the donor?'" he said in the HubSpot webinar mentioned earlier. To address these issues, companies and organizations, from Ford and IBM to the American Red Cross and Bread for the World, have created social media policies. These policies give clear cut guidelines on what can and cannot be shared publicly (on social media and other communication channels), whether employees can post as "themselves" or as official company spokespeople, and even how much time an employee can spend on social media.

Whether or not you create a policy is up to your organization's management team, the nature of your work, and the size of your organization. To determine if your organization needs a set policy or a more loosely structured set of guidelines, we recommend your team ask yourselves the following questions:

- Is your work sensitive in nature? Do you need to contend with local laws or culture? What is your organization's liability should an employee post something questionable? What processes do you have in place should a mistake happen – e.g. an employee posts something sensitive or questionable?

- What is the size of your organization and where are you located? Do you have one office or many around the world? What is your organizational culture like?

- Is your brand well recognized? How old or young is your brand? What is your brand's personality? What traits are already associated with your brand and will these be maintained and communicated through social media?

- Will staff and board members be able to post using personal accounts along with a statement saying they're connected to your organization but opinions are their own? Or do you want them to post only under your brand name?

- Will you allow employees and staff to "friend" or become personally connected with constituents? What happens if the employee leaves your organization for another?

- How will you communicate your social media policy or guidelines? Will you train employees and staff to use social media within the context of your brand?

As you can see from the questions, a social media policy is dependent on your organization and its unique culture, needs, mission, size and location. How you craft your policy – and how lenient or strict you'll be – is up to you or your management team. Do your research, discuss the questions with your team, and pick and choose what works best for your organization, brand, and culture. Consider that, in an age where social media is playing a notable part in many organizations' cultures – and donor and fundraising acquisition strategies – it makes sense to give your staff members and employees the freedom and ability to connect with constituents, share the joy of helping others, and spread the message about your cause – while also protecting your brand and organization.

**Inbound Marketing in Action: St. Baldrick's Creates Online Community Through Facebook**

"We knew we should be on Facebook," says Kristen Thies, Digital Communications Strategy Manager, for St. Baldrick's Foundation, "but in our beginning years we struggled with how to use this tool most effectively. Our problem, now that we have hindsight, is that we approached Facebook from a marketing 'talk to' perspective versus an inbound perspective."

Established as a nonprofit in 2005 and based in Monrovia, California, St. Baldrick's raises awareness and funds for childhood cancer research. The organization started using Facebook in 2009 in order to create an online community for volunteers and fundraising participants. Following "best practices," the marketing team posted multiple times a day – everyday. It was hard to tell what was working, and what wasn't – are Likes really all that matter?

Kristen took over the Facebook Page in July of 2012. "After struggling to 'get' Facebook for so long, something really clicked for us – and that was, we needed to create content that people love and want to share."

As part of their shift in mindset, Kristen and her team made the bold decision to post less. "By posting multiple times a day – whether we needed to or not – we were contributing to noise," she says. "Our followers had to determine, 'Should I pay attention to this post or can I ignore it?'" The decision was made to post only when the organization had something noteworthy to share. Says Kristen, "You really need courage to do this as it goes against much of what others will tell you. I really see this as quality over quantity."

The team also cut posts down to three lines or less. "Part of our problem is that we were really long-winded – posts were five,

116

six, seven lines. When you're scrolling through your newsfeed, that's a lot of information to digest." According to Kristen, she loves it when she can get a post down to one or two lines.

Because visuals play such an important role on Facebook, the St. Baldrick's team revamped their images to make them much more appealing, higher quality and to match the formatting standards of Facebook. According to Kristen, it's important to create visuals that match your brand – and that will add to the visual presentation of your Facebook Page.

Status updates generally feature the organization's blog posts with a compelling image – which is where Kristen and her team made the biggest change. Before their revamp, the team would post what Kristen calls "link posts": they would write the post text and then attach the blog link. Now, however, Kristen and her team use a high-quality visual that fits Facebook dimensions, a comment that's three lines or less, and a bit.ly URL. "Using the compelling photo post with a shortened link in the comment increased engagement twofold," she says.

To measure the effectiveness of their content, Kristen and her team began using campaign tracking through Google Analytics. They could see who was coming to their site from Facebook, but not from their own Facebook efforts specifically, so they began adding campaign tracking to each link posted using Google's URL builder. Using this tool, the team creates a tracking link and then shortens it with bit.ly; the bit.ly URL is then used in the post.

"With this method," says Kristen, "we were able to see that our Facebook content drove x number of visitors to the site for a specific month, and of those visitors we received x donations and x participant registrations. We could even see data for specific posts – for example, one post resulted in five donations and two registrations."

The community feedback with regard to these changes has been very good. One, the Page now has over 65,000 fans. Two, the quality of the conversation has improved and people now respond to posts with personal comments. Due to their success, the St. Baldrick's team is now looking for new strategies to take on, including how to continue to better measure metrics.

For nonprofits just starting out on Facebook, Kristen advises the following: Incorporate Facebook strategies with your website and email strategies (icons, Facebook shares, etc.). Give your brand a voice and personality with different types of content. She also advises that you test the best time of day to post updates. "We learned, through experimentation, that early morning posts work best for us – and this may due to the fact that we're West Coast. When we post at 6:00 AM, it's 9:00 AM on the East Coast. "

"We're really proud of what we've done," says Kristen. "We've created a real online community. The number of fans is good, of course, but it's not the end all, be all. What we love is that we're having conversations with our community of volunteers, as well as the childhood cancer community at large. It's a wonderful feeling – and why we're here to begin with."

**To Do:**

1. Create a social media strategy if your organization doesn't have one and share it with your executive team.

2. Open a Facebook or Twitter account for your organization if you don't have one.

3. Intermediate: Find ways for your executive team to get involved so that they begin to see the value of social media.

4. _____

5. _____

# Chapter 6

# Turn Strangers Into Supporters with Calls-to-Action

Attracting people to your website is the foundation for the Inbound Marketing Methodology – once you have it working for you, you're now ready to move to the second stage of the Methodology: Connecting. At this stage, you want ask people to connect with your organization – thus turning them from strangers into known supporters. You do this by collecting people's names and email addresses using calls-to-action, landing pages and forms – all three of which work together. Calls-to-action also drive deeper engagement with existing supporters, and they inspire advocacy across your entire constituency throughout the third and fourth stages (Engage and Inspire, respectively) of the Methodology. In this chapter, you'll learn where and when to use CTAs plus strategies for improving conversions.

## The inbound marketing call-to-action defined

Used in all types of marketing – from traditional to inbound – calls-to-action play an important role for getting people to take the next step in building a relationship with your organization, whether it's becoming a donor, fundraiser, member, volunteer or advocate. How do inbound CTAs differ from traditional marketing CTAs? When you send out a direct mail package, you're sending it to a list you've either purchased or compiled over many years. While you may not know all of the individuals on this list, it is a list of "known" prospects. With inbound marketing, you're attracting *unknown* people to your website through SEO, your blog and social media. If you have no way to capture their contact information, *they'll remain unknown* and all of your "attraction" work will be for naught. As an inbound nonprofit, you'll use CTAs to compel website visitors to want to connect with you by giving you their contact information.

An inbound call-to-action can be relatively simple, such as "read this article" or "sign up for our e-newsletter." Or, it can ask that people take actions that require effort, energy or even money: "sign this petition," "start a fundraising campaign" or "purchase our exclusive event t-shirt."

Inbound marketing calls-to-action (CTA) are often presented as a brightly colored button or captivating image with a text overlay. This visual contrast helps make the CTA more distinct and obvious to the visitor.

*Figure 1: Livestrong's CTA, "Get Started," segments visitors by market*

A powerful and contextual CTA compels people to want to give you their information in exchange for something of value to them. Once visitors to your website fill out a form and provides you with their contact information, you now know who that person is and can begin building a relationship through relevant and engaging content (i.e. emails about future causes, events, news about the impact of donations, etc.).

**Primary versus secondary calls-to-action**

Calls-to-action can be incorporated into almost any inbound marketing tactic, including your website, blog posts, emails, and social media updates. When creating your CTAs, think through the behaviors you want people to take when they arrive at your website or read your emails or social media updates. Think of CTAs as gently nudging people in the direction you want them to go. But, what if you want people to take two or more actions – such as fill out a petition *and* follow you on social media? Can you do that? The answer is, yes!

When people come to your organization's website, you most likely have a main action you want them to take: register, donate, get involved, download something, etc. This is your primary call-to-action. But, you may also have other actions you want them to take: follow on social media, read an article, etc. These are your secondary CTAs. By combining primary and secondary CTAs, you can prioritize, balance and support your organization's marketing goals. They also help you move people to want to connect with you in ways that make them feel comfortable. Let's say, for example, a person comes to your website. He or she may not be ready to donate, fundraise or get involved (your primary CTA). But, just because this person isn't ready to take an action today doesn't mean you should let them leave your site without taking a small step toward connecting with you. This is where secondary CTAs come into play: you can ask people to read a blog article or story (thus educating them and maybe even inspiring them to take the next step in terms of giving, joining, etc.), subscribe to your blog or e-newsletter, or follow you on social media. While the primary CTA is more prominent, the secondary CTA is there for those not ready to take your most desired action.

The beauty of primary and secondary calls-to-action is that they're like a good jacket that changes roles depending on your purpose. To wear a jacket to a meeting, men can add trousers and a tie, or women a blouse and jewelry. Switch out the trousers and the tie for jeans or a mini-skirt and strappy sandals and you're ready to party. Primary and secondary CTAs work the same way – each CTA's role (and how many you need) depends on the context and your goals. Your website homepage may have three, four or five CTAs. DoSomething.org, for example, has a primary CTA on its home page for saving music education programs (Figure 1). The secondary CTAs ask people to become a member of the organization or to follow the organization on social media. While the navigational links across the top of the page are static; the organization's primary and secondary CTAs are subject to change.

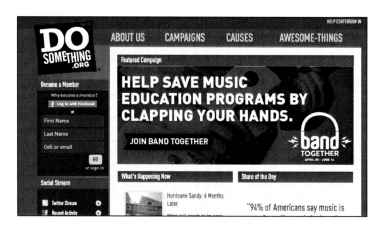

*Figure 1: DoSomething.org's home page showing primary and secondary CTAs*

To effectively use primary and secondary CTAs together, you want to make sure your secondary CTA complements your primary CTA rather than competing with it or overpowering it. Your audience should know immediately what is your desired course of action. The one place where you do not want a secondary CTA is on your landing pages (which we'll cover in the next chapter). The sole purpose of a landing page is to get people to provide you with their contact information by filling out a form in exchange for something;

multiple calls-to-action on a landing page distract people and will lower your conversion rates.

**Determine the actions you want people to take**

You can use CTAs to encourage website visitors or e-newsletter readers to take a primary action, such as to register, donate, volunteer, become a member, etc. Or, you can use CTAs to simply ask people to read your stories and/or share them on social media. The beauty of calls-to-action, whether primary or secondary, is that you can use them in many different ways to achieve a desired result. When creating your strategy for any piece of content, it pays to ask first, "What action do we want people to take?" Work through what you want people to do: Open the newsletter → read the article → Share the article. Or, Visit website → sign up for fundraising campaign → email personal network and ask them to donate.

To be really effective, build your calls-to-action based on your personas – and then work through why you're asking people to take the action. For example, when new prospective fundraisers come to your homepage, what do you want them to do? Ditto for active and past fundraisers. Or, when a new prospective donor comes to your homepage and isn't ready to give, what do you want this person to do? What actions do you want recurring donors or lost donors to take? The same questions apply for volunteers and for people who may be prospective members.

## Creating CTAs that convert

Clearly articulating your ideas, so that they resonate with and capture the attention of your audience, is key when it comes to effective inbound marketing – and crucial when it comes to creating CTAs. If your CTA doesn't compel people to take the next step – meaning, it doesn't convert them – then it's failed in its job. In the for-profit world, "conversion" is often defined in terms of sales or product or service inquiries. As a nonprofit, you'll use conversion in a similar way – except you're working to achieve different outcomes – advocacy, volunteering, donating, fundraising, etc. To ensure the highest conversion rates for your CTAs, you'll want to focus on three strategies that will help attract website visitors to click through and convert: copy, design, and testing.

## Use clear, succinct language

The most basic step to creating compelling CTAs is to clearly describe *why* you want people to take the desired action. Your "why" may be that when a website visitor is inspired to take action, he or she is impacting the world in a favorable way. For example, you're helping to end hunger when you donate 10 jars of peanut butter to DoSomething.org's Peanut Butter and Jam Slam! (Figure 2).

*Figure 2: DoSomething.org's call-to-action explains that those who donate will help end hunger in the U.S.*

The other central element of a great CTA is the *action* you want people to take – or in other words, the verb. We recommend you create a list of snappy verbs that suggest actions to the reader: "Sign up," "Enroll," "Donate" "Choose," "Help," "Save," "Run," "Walk," "Jump," "Ride," "Learn," "Act" "Sign," etc. The American Red Cross, for example, has a terrific CTA on its homepage that's clear and succinct: "Get CPR and First Aid Certified – Enroll Now" (Figure 3).

And, notice the secondary CTA directly beneath the main CTA:

"Download Red Cross Apps for safety information at your fingertips."

*Figure 3: American Red Cross CTA*

You can also use numbers to help move people to action. Numbers break through the clutter of ambiguity and define expectations. For Nothing But Nets (Figure 4), the CTA shows a 1:1 correlation: "Send a Net. Save a Life." The CTA also explains how just $10 can save one life from malaria. Use numbers to show impact: lives saved, resources given, dollars raised, etc.

Figure 4: Nothing But Nets CTA showing 1:1 correlation

When crafting your CTAs, keep them short and to the point, generally 90 to 150 characters. The CTA on Heartwaves' home page is a great example: "Start your Heartwaves page now" (Figure 5). We recommend that you write out your CTA using a few full sentences and then remove the words that don't contribute to your core message.

*Figure 5: Heartwaves succinct CTA*

**Use design to capture attention**

The goal of your call-to-action is to attract the attention of website visitors and have them ultimately click on the CTA. One way to convey the importance of your CTA and call attention to it is to enlarge it and/or incorporate buttons, unconventional shapes, arrows, or contrasting colors. A good tip for increasing conversions is to use CTA copy on the button itself: "Donate," "Register Now," etc. versus using the less effective and vague "Submit" or "Learn More." Where you place your CTA on the page is also important. Placing it "above the fold" so that viewers don't have to scroll down to view it can help increase conversions. To get people to read a story about its equine ambulance rescue service, for example, the MSPCA placed the CTA –along with a captivating photo! – on its homepage in the "slider" at the top of the page (Figure 6).

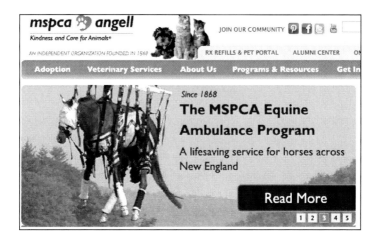

*Figure 6: MSPCA's home page CTA to read a story*

**Test your CTAs**

You can find a wealth of information regarding marketing best practices but sometimes, these "best practices" aren't what's best for your organization. To ensure your CTAs (and other marketing tactics) are performing optimally, it pays to test – everything! You can test copy, design, placement, images and the offer. The way inbound marketers test elements is through A/B testing.

To perform an A/B test, create two versions of your call-to-action – with one specific element changed (the element you're testing). Version A, for example, may have a red button while Version B has a blue button. Standard A/B testing tools will display your variations to website visitors and will then keep track of the conversions separately for you to compare after a period of time (usually around two to four weeks, depending on the volume of traffic). At the end of the testing period, you'll know which color had a higher conversion rate. If the red button "won," you can then use the red button and begin testing the copy on the button itself. When performing A/B tests, you want to test one variable at a time – meaning, you don't want to test both the copy and the color of a button – so that you know exactly which element is triggering the response you want.

**Inbound Marketing In Action: DoSomething.Org Uses CTAs to Get Millennials to Take Action**

Founded in 1993 by activist and actor Andrew Shue, DoSomething.org is one of the largest organizations for young people and social change in the U.S. The organization began when Shue heard President Clinton say that in order to give back, one could start anywhere with small actions. Shue, playing the role of Billy Campbell on *Melrose Place*, asked director Aaron Spelling for one minute of time in order to encourage the show's young audience to become active citizens and leaders.

The organization's current CEO and Chief Old Person, Nancy Lublin, who founded Dress for Success in 1996, took over in 2003 and has grown the organization to where it is today. "We're all about reaching young people where they are," explains Naomi Hirabayashi, the organization's Chief Marketing Officer. "We want to attract the student sitting in the middle or back of the class and show them how community service and social action can be easy and fun. We want them to learn their 'small' actions can and do make a difference."

The organization is roughly 90 percent funded through corporate partners – allowing DoSomething.org to offer scholarship drawings to young people when they get involved in campaigns. "We never, ever ask our social action volunteers for even five cents," says Naomi. "Some teenagers may not have an allowance and college students may be on very tight budgets. Instead of asking for money, we ask them to do something."

One such "something" is their annual Teens for Jeans campaign, which runs each January. A national cause campaign, Teens for Jeans rallies young people across the U.S. to donate gently used jeans at their local Aéropostale store to benefit homeless teens in need. The call-to-action is simple: "Any day in

January, go to your local Aéropostale store and drop off your gently used jeans. DoSomething.org will reallocate the jeans to a local homeless youth in the store's area." DoSomething.org gives young people resources, such as flyers, banners, and action guides, on how to host successful Teens for Jeans drives in their communities, schools, etc.

According to Naomi, the marketing team came up with idea six years ago using data. "The top pages on our site have to do with poverty and homelessness – these are two of the top five concerns young people care about," she says. In order to determine what homeless shelters actually needed, the team created a "massive" national database manually and then called shelters. The number one requested item? Jeans. "'Jeans' is something simple – an article of clothing that every young person should own," says Naomi, "and something that doesn't have be to washed every day."

DoSomething.org then cold-called national retailer Aéropostale and pitched them on the idea of a national jean drive. "From a business perspective, it made sense," says Naomi. "January is a slow month for retailers. Having young people drop off used jeans at stores brought in extra foot traffic around a seasonally low time. Teens for Jeans is the perfect campaign because the young people are happy with the impact they've made; the shelters are happy because they get needed clothing to help homeless teens in need; the parents are happy because the teens are cleaning out the closets; and our partner Aéropostale is happy because they see increased foot traffic and they're the lead partner on a powerful cause marketing campaign. Everyone wins."

In 2013, the campaign drove over 900,000 pairs of donated jeans, which will clothe one out two teens in the U.S. To date, young people have donated 3.5 million pairs of jeans through Teens for Jeans.

For this campaign (and others), Naomi and her team get the word out to their audience in three ways: owned media (DoSomething.org channels), earned media (PR), and donated media (marketing partners). Campaign calls-to-action are impactful, fun and shareable and include snapping photos of jean drives and uploading them to the website as well as sharing them on social media. (You can view the impact of the 2013 and previous campaigns, including photos and videos, at dosomething.org/jeansforteens.) "What we do," says Naomi, "is take big causes that can be overwhelming to young people and break them down into actionable steps. We make doing good accessible for young people by meeting them where they are and providing simple, measurable and meaningful calls-to-action on causes they care about."

**To Do:**

1. Tie one CTA on your homepage to each persona (i.e. Volunteers, Donors, Corporate Sponsors).

2. Read HubSpot's *101 Examples of CTAs* for ideas on how to improve your CTAs: **http://offers.hubspot.com/101-examples-of-effective-calls-to-action**

3. Intermediate: Test the text on a primary call-to-action for 1 month (i.e. Donate vs. Give now)

4. _____

5. _____

# Chapter 7
# Capture Prospective Supporter's Information with Landing Pages

One of the biggest mistakes organizations make, when asking people to take a specific action, is to send them directly to their website's homepage from an email, blog post or social media update. The problem with this approach is that if you've piqued people's attention on one specific topic and they click through to your general homepage, they won't find what they're looking for right away – or the content won't be relevant to their previous piece of content. Sending people to your homepage can cause visitors to either spend wasted time looking around your website to find what they're looking for or simply leave. It pays, therefore, to develop landing pages – hyper focused by topic or persona – to accompany your calls-to-action.

138

By sending your visitors to a targeted landing page, you're directing them to the exact place they need to be to fill out a form and obtain the information they're seeking or complete the action they intended to after they clicked the call-to-action that brought them to the landing page. This "conversion path," as it's called, keeps visitors from wandering around your website looking for that eBook or event you promoted to them, getting distracted, and clicking back out – without giving you their contact information!

A well-crafted landing page matches the call-to-action to which it's associated. Figure 1 shows one of the primary calls-to-action on The Urban Alternative's homepage for a book written by Lois Evans, the wife of founder Tony Evans. When you click on the CTA, you're taken to a landing page (Figure 2) where you fill out a form (and give a donation in any amount) in order to receive the book. As you can see, the CTA on the homepage matches the offer on the landing page – a book by Lois Evans. If a different offer were presented, you, as the visitor, would get confused and maybe even a little peeved, and would most likely leave the website. Ensuring your landing page matches the CTA significantly improves conversion rates – that is, getting people to fill out the landing page form so you're able to educate and nurture them throughout the lifetime of engagement with your organization (you'll learn about

nurturing in Chapter 9).

*Figure 1: The Urban Alternative Homepage (book by Lois Evans*

*outlined)*

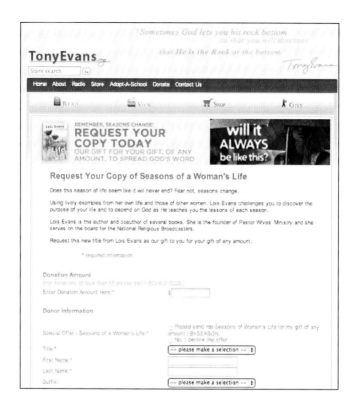

*Figure 2: The landing page for the Lois Evan's book*

## Building effective landing pages

Optimized landing pages – that is, those that have a high view-to-submission conversion rate – employ a number of strategies that make them effective. Each element on the page, from the headline to the form, has a purpose and helps with getting the visitor to take action. In the section that follows, you'll find ten strategies for creating effective landing pages.

**Strategy #1: Anchor people with the headline**

The headline, which is usually the first thing visitors see when they arrive on your landing page, lets people know they've arrived at the right place ("Oh good, this is the eBook I wanted"). Because people's attention spans are very short – the average online attention span is eight seconds – your headline needs to be as clear and concise as possible. You need to ensure people understand what you're asking them to do or what they'll get if they take your desired action as soon as they "land" on your page. In Figure 3, the Vermont College of Fine Arts gives people seven "mind-blowing" reasons for learning more about their Master of Fine Arts program in music. The headline is clear and concise and the reader knows what he/she will get when downloading the offer.

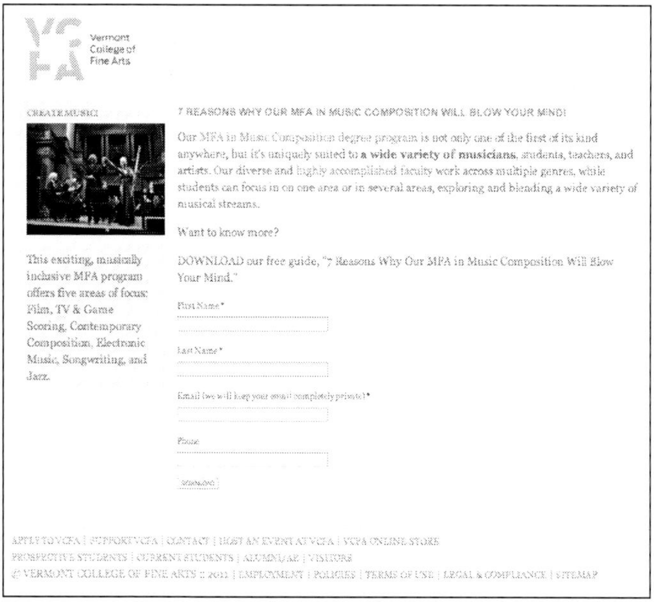

*Figure 3: Vermont College of Fine Arts landing page with headline*

**Strategy #2: Explain the benefit of taking action**

As a nonprofit, not all of your landing pages will be geared toward offering people an informational piece of content. Instead, you'll want to compel people to fundraise, donate, volunteer, register, attend, etc. Your landing page content should explain – as concisely as possible – what people will get when they choose to take the requested action and fill out the form. What they'll "get" may not be tangible. Instead, it may be the effect of helping your cause; for example, "Your $10 donation helps build a well, end hunger, find

143

a cure," etc. You'll want to highlight the benefits of taking the desired action with a brief paragraph or a few bullet points. Your copy should emphasize how taking the action addresses the specific problem, need, or interest your constituents care about.

**Strategy #3: Grab attention with a visual**

Relevant images or graphics instantly attract your readers' attention and reinforce the benefits detailed in your landing page copy. Because 90 percent of information transmitted to the brain is visual, and because we process visuals 60,000 times faster than we do text, incorporating an image on your landing page is an effective way to entice visitors and convey the purpose of your landing page – as well as reinforce why they should take the requested action. For example, if you were building a landing page for an eBook, you could include an image of the eBook cover to illustrate what your visitors will get when they fill out your form. Or, you can simply use images that communicate what the request is about – as DoSomething.org did with their Peanut Butter and Jam Slam showcased in Chapter Six.

If you are looking for original, captivating images, consider using Flickr's free Creative Commons images with a simple photo credit instead of stock images. Many of these images are captivating and much more true to "real life" (e.g they're not staged). They also won't be found on every other landing page.

**Strategy #4: Keep your layout clean and simple**

The layout of your landing page should guide visitors through the page to the form. Strive to convey the top three or four most important pieces of information first. Use bullet points, numbering, and bold or italicized text to simplify the visual layout and highlight the main points. You want to create a page format that makes it easy for visitors to understand what you're asking them to do and the benefits of providing you with their contact information on the form. One good practice is to ask people outside of your organization or marketing team to view your landing page. Do they understand what you want them to do in less than five seconds? Called the "blink test," this test is a good way to make sure your landing pages are clear and concise – and that potential constituents "get" what you want them to do. Depending on the length of your page copy, you'll want to include the form, either to the right of or directly beneath the copy.

**Strategy #5: Keep forms above the fold**

The key element on your landing page, the form is the place where the conversion takes place. It's important, therefore, to keep the form above the fold so that it's immediately visible. How long should you make your form – or rather, how many fields should you include? The length of your form is always a tradeoff between the quantity and quality of the contact information you'd like to collect. More people are likely to fill out a shorter form, but you won't capture as much desired information. Fewer people will fill out a longer form, but you'll have more information to work with when you begin segmenting your contacts for nurturing.

Also take into consideration the context in which you're using the form. If you're asking people to subscribe to your blog or e-newsletter, you may want to keep your form to a minimum and ask only for an email address. If you're asking people to register for an event or to purchase something, then your form will be longer and will include things such as credit card information, a phone number, t-shirt size, etc. Big Brothers Big Sisters, for example, uses a longer form when asking people to volunteer (Figure 4).

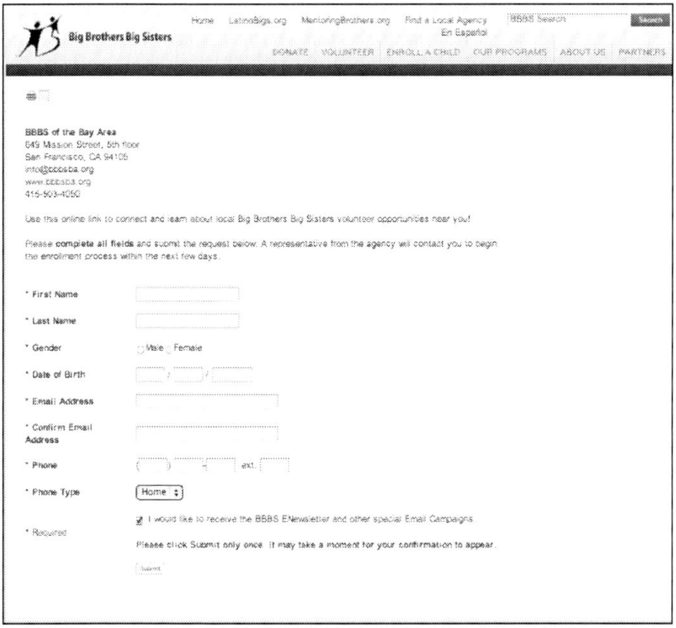

*Figure 4: Volunteer registration form for Big Brothers Big Sisters*

## Strategy #6: Make your buttons "action-oriented"

The last component of your landing page shouldn't be overlooked: your call-to-action button. On most landing page forms, the default text on the call-to-action button is "Submit," which data show results in low conversion rates. "Submit" also doesn't convey what the person gets when they click the button. To improve conversions, make your buttons engaging and relevant to your offer. A/B test your buttons with different wording and default to the one with the highest conversion rate. Putting more thought into your

147

button text can significantly affect how people respond.  Try "Register Today" or "Subscribe Now."

**Strategy #7: Remove navigational elements**

As we explained earlier, the main goal of your landing page is to get your visitors to fill out your forms and become "known" visitors, whilst providing them with relevant content that will further connect them to your organization. You've attracted them to your landing page, and now you want to keep them there so that they'll take the desired action. To reduce the likelihood of page visitors clicking away to other parts of your website, consider removing all navigation and links from the landing page. This means you remove the top or side-level navigation and any sidebar or footer links. The only thing people will see is your landing page copy, your compelling image, and the form (Figure 5).

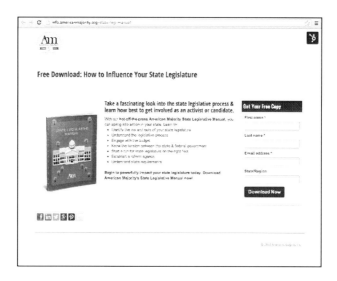

*Figure 5: An example of a landing page with navigational elements removed*

By removing all navigational elements, you eliminate any distractions that might keep visitors from completing your form and help ensure more visitors actually fill it out. Most landing page tools have this option to remove navigation.

One exception exists to this rule: You can and should include a link to your privacy policy page. Your privacy policy page will help answer any questions your visitors may have about how you're going to use their information. It also increases the likelihood of them filling out your form. Remember, you want your visitors to see you as transparent, credible and trustworthy. Make sure your privacy policy backs it up. If you don't have a privacy policy, but are collecting personal information, we highly encourage you to create one.

**Strategy #8: Keep branding consistent**

When developing your landing pages, be sure to keep the same look and feel of your website and keep the language, colors, text, and logos uniform on all pages. By maintaining brand consistency, you'll add credibility to your landing pages and increase the likelihood of visitors filling out the landing page form.

**Strategy #9: Create mobile optimized pages**

As the 2012 Millennial Impact Report shows, having a mobile optimized site is essential when reaching out to Millennials – and that goes for your landing pages as well. When developing your pages, be sure all content is in HTML rather than Flash (which doesn't work on iPhones or iPads) or contained inside images. (The default for many email programs, including Gmail, is "images off." Content inside images isn't seen unless the person clicks, "Show images.") Also consider shorter headlines: a headline with six or more words looks crowded on the smaller screen where size is at a premium. You'll also want to use simpler forms with fewer fields.

Research already proves that longer forms lower conversion – this is even more so on a mobile device where people "scan and delete."

**Strategy #10: Test, test, test!**

And finally, use A/B testing to test the various elements on your landing page the way you test calls-to-action. As mentioned, you can test your headlines, images, form lengths, and call-to-action buttons. But make sure to only test one detail at a time. As discussed in Chapter 6, best practices for one organization may not be a best practice for your organization.

**The form has been submitted, now what?**

Once your website visitors have filled out your form, you then want to direct them to a "thank you" page. On this page you'll include a link to download any information piece. Or, your thank you page could be the receipt of a donation, confirmed event registration, or simply a "thank you." You can also include links to your social media pages or blog and any secondary call-to-action.

**Why a "Contact Us" form isn't a landing page**

It's easy to let your "Contact Us" form serve double duty as a way to gather people's contact information. Unfortunately, it's not the best strategy. One, Contact Us forms are rarely tied to a valuable offer or an inbound marketing campaign; two, they're usually hidden under "About Us"; and three, they frequently attract spam and sales people. "Contact Us" forms also limit your ability to attract potential constituents using content tied to your personas. You can keep your Contact Us form as a way for people to ask you questions or to inquire about other types of information but we recommend you don't use them as a way to build your inbound marketing database.

**Inbound Marketing In Action: Urban Alternative Realizes 83% Land Page Conversion Rate**

A Christian-based nonprofit, Tony Evans' The Urban Alternative ministry (**www.tonyevans.org**) reaches millions of people around the globe. Dr. Evans' outreach includes both a radio show and TV show broadcast through 850 outlets globally. In addition to radio and TV, people from 126 nations access the organization's website where they can download and/or purchase inspirational and devotional DVDs, CDs, books, and eBooks. Says Eric Allen, Program Manager, in a bit of understatement, "We have a very large funnel to manage." Indeed.

According to Eric, faith-based nonprofits comprise 32 percent – or $95.8 billion annually – of charitable giving. "For the

Urban Alternative, and for many Christian nonprofits, it's all about content," says Eric. "We've had to change our entire mindset due to the Internet and all of the free content now available. Before, we charged money for our products. This gave us a set price point but it also meant fewer sales as we were 'competing' with the free content available elsewhere. We've now moved to a premium-based system. If someone calls in or responds online with a donation, he or she receives a gift: a CD series, a book, etc. With a premium-based system, we have far more people in our funnel but the amount of the donation is lower. So the challenge has become, how do we manage all these names and how do we encourage people to come back and donate again?"

Another challenge faced by The Urban Alternative was their reliance on a legacy system to manage their email and contacts database. According to Eric, the nonprofit needed a more robust system that allowed them to develop integrated email campaigns tied to landing pages – as well as analytics telling them how their campaigns were performing. "We had no idea how people were reacting to our content," says Eric.

The nonprofit signed on to HubSpot in 2012 – and the effect was immediate. "We put together a campaign, which included a free download on overcoming spiritual warfare and living a life of victory. We got an 85 percent conversion rate. It was amazing! Even HubSpot called us because they were amazed!" Today this landing page continues to generate a 39 percent conversion rate (see Figure 6).

*Figure 6: The Urban Alternative's landing page that generated an 85% response rate.*

The Urban Alternative realizes an average conversion rate of 25 – 30 percent for many of its offers and campaigns, such as the 30 Days to Financial Victory email campaign (go.tonyevans.org/financial-victory). With this campaign, recipients receive money management tips as well as spiritual advice for 30 days.

Knowing the analytics behind each campaign helps Eric and his team create other relevant offers that consistently move people through the giving cycle. The organization sends people devotions and other materials which helps keep the nonprofit top-of-mind for when they send their year-end appeal.

When asked if he had advice for other faith-based nonprofits regarding inbound marketing, Eric shared these three tips. One, explore what inbound marketing means for your organization. Look at what are your touch-points and what content can you repurpose. Christian nonprofits especially, he says, should have a wealth of content on hand – sermons, research, etc. – that can be dusted off and repurposed to help tell your story. "Our financial victory campaign, for example, came from sermons Dr. Evans gave back in the 1990s. We repurposed these into a booklet and then repurposed that into a conversion campaign."

Two, take what works in the secular world and put it to use in the sacred. "When we first started with HubSpot, the whole idea of inbound marketing made my head spin," says Eric. "We had no idea what was meant by a 'lead' or how the methods used to turn people into customers by for-profit companies could be used for nonprofits and their donors – especially ours, since we're religious based." Eric and his team learned how to use inbound marketing tactics to develop and harvest names and to create a donor file that helps support the mission of the organization. "With inbound marketing, we're able to bring people back to our organization, and over time, move them to give bigger donations."

And three get your story heard and understood! Says Eric, "As a faith-based organization, we're reaching people in their cars, at schools and churches, and throughout communities. It's really important that people not only hear us, but understand our story – and the impact their donations have in helping us achieve our mission." Eric and his team can tell that story and then use inbound marketing tactics to ensure their constituents – and prospective constituents – hear it, too.

**To Do:**

1. Take 3 of the above strategies and optimize your landing pages.

2. Intermediate: Take an existing offer, like "Contact Us to Volunteer" or "Download our 2012 Annual Report" and create a landing page with a form for it.

3. _____

4. _____

5. _____

# Part Four

# **Engage**

*"Fundraising is not an event; it is a process."*
***-Edgar D. Powell***

# Chapter 8
# Educate Supporters Through Email Marketing

In our Introduction, we related a story about how our CEO, Brian Halligan, uses Gmail's Priority Inbox to filter his mail. Priority Inbox is a pretty cool tool. In case you've never heard of it or don't use it, the tool automatically sorts your mail for you based on your set preferences. The important stuff, *from people and brands you like*, rises to the top. Everything else, including the stuff from people and brands you don't like (re: ignore), falls into the "regular" inbox. Gmail users tend to live in their Priority Inbox because that's where the information they most want to read resides. The email in the regular box tends to pile up; research from Google shows that Gmail users then either delete this email or archive it – without reading it – in one fell swoop.

While not everyone uses Gmail or even the Priority Inbox, how we "triage" our email is still the same. Whether you're viewing email on your phone or your desktop, you most likely skim through the sender names and subject lines – quickly archiving or deleting the stuff you don't want or need to read. In other words, we filter email based on whether it comes from people and brands we like – or don't like. The key take-away for you? To be an effective inbound nonprofit, it's important that your email marketing is relevant, personalized, and most importantly, loveable.

An important part of the "Engage" stage of the Inbound Marketing Methodology, email marketing is what drives people to move further down the marketing funnel with your organization. Inbound nonprofits use email to nurture relationships and build trust with their constituents. With email marketing, you help keep awareness of your cause or organization top-of-mind while also encouraging people to become more and more connected to your mission.

"But," you may be thinking, "*How* do we do this? My email inbox is overflowing! Most of what I get is junk!" Exactly! Rather than sending one-size-fits-some messages, inbound nonprofits send the right message to the right people at the right time – which is what you'll learn in this chapter.

**Effective email marketing starts with an opt-in list**

As a nonprofit, you may have purchased lists in the past in order to send fundraising appeals through the mail. The problem with purchased lists is that they're comprised of people who didn't ask to receive information from your organization – that's why most direct mail is often thrown immediately into the recycle bin. While the appeal may be heartfelt, the message itself isn't relevant to the recipient.

With an inbound email marketing strategy, on the other hand, the key concept is "opt in." Inbound marketing tactics, such as SEO, blogging and social media, attract visitors to your website – visitors who have an interest in your cause or organization. Once they arrive, you use calls-to-action to drive individuals to landing pages where you collect their contact information, including email addresses. When people opt-in this way, they've taken the first step in saying, "Yes, I want to begin a relationship with your organization." Your house opt-in list, then, is pure gold because it's made up of people who have shown interest in your organization. In fact, in one MarketingSherpa study, 40 percent of marketers stated their opt-in email lists drove ninety percent of ROI – more than search and PPC! We'll go through tips to grow your opt-in list shortly.

**Make your content relevant – segment your list**

According to the report, "10 Facts About How and Why Consumers Like and Subscribe," from Chadwick Martin Bailey, a Boston market research company, people unsubscribe from email lists for two reasons: they receive too many emails (69%) and the content isn't relevant (56%). MarketingSherpa's 2011 "Marketing Wisdom" report showed similar data: four out of ten email subscribers reported they marked emails as spam because the communication was irrelevant. The same report noted that emails tailored to specific audiences through segmentation got *fifty percent more clicks than non-segmented emails.*

Despite the data – and the wealth of information on why it's more effective to create content tailored to specific audiences – many organizations continue to send the same tired "email blast" to their entire list of major donors, regular donors, volunteers, members, advocates, and fundraisers. When your constituents receive these types of blast emails, they begin to tune you out, delete your irrelevant email without reading it, unsubscribe from your list – or worse, report your email as spam.

To avoid these scenarios, you must segment your email list. For most nonprofits, this means you'll most likely have the following groups (some of your constituents will fall into multiple groups; that's ok): donors (segment further by new, recurring and past), members, fundraisers, volunteers and staff members, and partners and sponsors. (Your various personas, which we discussed in Chapter Two, come into play within each group). Once your list is segmented, it's much easier to provide content tailored to each group – content that's relevant and that people will want to read and share with others.

**Create content tailored to your groups**

In order to execute an effective communication strategy between your organization and its constituents, you must first determine how and when to communicate with each group of individuals. The key to successful email marketing is to tailor your emails to your specific personas. Generally, nonprofits send five types of emails: emails about your organization, information about events, internal updates and e-newsletters, thank you emails, and emails to major donors and sponsors. This content doesn't need to be drastically different, but it should speak to each group individually.

**Type #1: Emails that update people about your organization**

Many organizations choose to send weekly or monthly digests to keep their supporters or fan base current on events, goals, and future plans. These type of "informational" messages may not be as fun or engaging as your fundraising or newsletter emails, but they do provide a wonderful opportunity to make a lasting first impression with new contacts while keeping your current supporters up-to-date with what you've been up to. Since these are more frequent, ask your subscribers to opt-into this type of email specifically. You can do this through a dedicated landing page.

To target these types of messages, send all new constituents a general overview of your organization and its mission once they first come on board; use future messages to educate each group separately about your cause and provide ways for them to get involved based on how they want to interact with your organization, whether it's donating or fundraising. For businesses that visit your website and show interest in your organization, let them know how they can contribute to your cause through sponsorship opportunities. Volunteers and/or members, too, can receive tailored messages about how to become more active or involved.

**Type #2: Emails promoting events**

Event emails are very effective because you can segment out your list by location and target those that can attend in-person first and then that can support online but not attend separately. The key to making this type of email work is to promote only one event per email. The email should be brief but descriptive enough to convey the purpose and value. Consider making use of formatting techniques such as bulleted lists, which can help you clearly describe the most important event information while avoiding long sentences that readers will only skim over and thus miss important details. In addition, you should use a large and attractive call-to-action in your email with clear language that directs your readers to an event-specific landing page to register or volunteer for the event as the next step.

Supporters and donors get an email that clearly explains the purpose of the event and the call-to-action. Sponsors get a different email that explains the sponsorship opportunities associated with the event. Volunteers and staff get an email about event logistics, roles, tasks, etc. And your partners should get an email that explains logistics, specific needs, and the overall fundraising goal. Partners need to know more about how the event will impact your long-term goals and mission in order to determine how they can help and what resources they can provide.

**Type #3: Emails about internal updates**

Many nonprofits, especially larger ones, send internal updates or newsletters to members, volunteers, and staff to let them know the latest about new projects, volunteering opportunities, upcoming events, or job openings. While members, volunteers, and staff may seem like separate groups, they should be categorized together as the people in each group work for your organization. It's important, therefore, to share the same internal information with these groups in order to ensure everyone is "on the same page" and to create camaraderie between your staff and volunteers. To keep these types of emails interesting, and your readers engaged, include fun topics, such as "volunteer of the month" or stories from volunteers out in the field – and don't forget to include photos of people that contribute and/or are featured.

**Type #4: Confirmation and thank you emails**

Set up thank you emails to go out automatically when someone makes an online donation. Be sure each thank you email is customized to the form and campaign – you don't want a donor to receive an email that should have gone to a prospective volunteer. In these emails, thank the individual for the donation and provide a short description of how his or her efforts will impact your organization and cause. Time these to go out a few hours after the donation is made. Most likely, you have an automated donation receipt going out immediately after the donation is made. The thank you email is a little more personal and comes from your organization, not the donation processor.

And, of course, you'll want to send your volunteers and fundraisers timely emails thanking them for their time and effort. While you can send an email targeted to this special group, you may also want to send personal emails to those volunteers who headed up a committee, oversaw an event or went above and beyond the call of duty.

**Type #5: Emails for high value donors and sponsors**

Every nonprofit has a shorter list of dedicated sponsors and major gift donors. Sometimes, you may want to send a dedicated email to this group. For example, if you're hosting an exclusive charity gala, you might want to send an email letting them know of any important event updates. These emails can lead to new sponsorship opportunities and large donation asks; they also encourage your most important sponsors and donors to promote your event or cause on your behalf. In addition, personalized emails to your top five or ten major donors are a great way to show your gratitude and further build relationships.

**Tips for growing your email list**

Your email list has a short shelf life. People change jobs, and even change names, and thus change their email address without telling you – making your email list less effective over time – the lifespan of an email address is approximately 16 months. Our research has shown that an average list retains only seventy-five percent of its members after one year – which means your list expires at a rate of twenty-five percent a year. If you're not replenishing your list with new prospective constituents on a regular basis, your list will eventually become worthless to your organization. Growing your opt-in list is limited only by your imagination – but to get you started, we've provided you with a few tips to implement today.

**Make your subscription box easy to find**

Whether you're asking people to subscribe to your blog or your e-newsletter, place your subscription form where it's very easy to see. Make it clearly stand out on your sidebar or on the upper part of your website's homepage so that visitors' eyes navigate toward it. Tell people what they'll get when they subscribe – e.g. weekly blog posts, email alerts, monthly newsletter, etc. Providing different options for frequency will increase the likelihood of someone opting in to your email list, and it also sets expectations of when and how often they'll be receiving your emails.

**Tie an offer to your opt-in list**

To sweeten the deal of subscribing, offer people additional value in the form of a "freemium": an eBook, special report, or webinar (to name a few things). Use A/B testing to see which "freemium" or free premium offers the most subscribers.

**Promote your email subscription offer on social media**

If you have a landing page for your email or blog subscription associated with a valuable piece of content, use this URL and a call-to-action on your social media profiles. You can also create an "opt in" tab on your Facebook Page as well as promote the offer on your other social media pages.

**Ask people to share or "forward" to a friend**

This tip is pretty simple and quite effective, but it's often overlooked. Because your subscribers are people who support your cause, you can ask them to email, tweet, or forward your emails to their colleagues, friends, and family.

To make this process easy, include sharing buttons for social media in your email as well as a "forward to a friend" button or link in each email. (If you use an email service provider, this function is often built into the email template. HubSpot's email tool also includes these features.) When people share with their networks, those connected to them are much more likely to may come to your website and subscribe because of the personal connection, versus total strangers.

**Consider partnerships with related nonprofits**

Another way to grow your list is to jointly market with a related nonprofit (or even a for-profit company that markets to nonprofits). Co-hosting webinars or creating ebooks or reports offers a couple of benefits: One, you reduce your workload as you now have additional people helping you create content (always a win-win!); two, you capitalize on each organization or company's existing reach and gain exposure to constituents who may not know about your organization yet. HubSpot does this with nonprofit customers to help them get started with their inbound marketing campaign each quarter.

**Optimize the unsubscribe process**

It's a fact of life: people will unsubscribe from your list. You can use the unsubscribe process to help change people's minds. One strategy is to give them options on the unsubscribe page. Ask if they'd rather receive fewer emails or particular types of emails (e.g. only major announcements or a monthly newsletter) rather than just unsubscribe altogether. You can also suggest alternative channels for engagement by providing links your social media pages.

**Optimize your emails for mobile viewing**

Over 40% of emails sent are read on mobile devices, so it's extremely important to make sure your email tool optimizes for mobile viewing automatically. You should also keep this in mind when composing you emails as to keep the content concise, as long paragraphs will look double the length on mobile phones. You can also design mobile templates for your emails on various email service providers. Keep mobile in mind when developing or optimizing your email strategy.

Once you have these tactics down, you can then begin thinking about nurturing your constituents through the giving cycle with what we call "lead nurturing. You'll learn more about the giving cycle and lead nurturing in the next chapter.

**To Do:**

1. Go through your existing email list. List three to five segments you want to start marketing to more effectively.

2. Create an e-newsletter subscription landing page to collect email addresses.

3. Intermediate: A/B test your call-to-action in your next email blast between volunteer and donate. See which results in more clicks.

4. _____

5. _____

# Chapter 9
# Move Prospects Through the "Funnel" with Lead Nurturing

Up until now, we've talked about how to attract, connect and engage people on your website through raising brand awareness and creating content that will inspire prospective supporters to provide you with their contact information. In the last chapter, we talked about using segmented email to reach out to your constituents with highly targeted content and different types of emails. But, what about the people who come to your website and subscribe to your blog or follow you on social media but don't take any other immediate action? What do you do with them – other than let them sit in your database? The answer is, you continue to nurture them so that over time, you move them through your marketing funnel and ultimately convert them into donors, members, fundraisers, etc. This marketing process is what's referred to as "lead nurturing" and it's what you'll learn in this chapter.

**Lead nurturing for the nonprofit**

Often referred to as "marketing automation," lead nurturing is a system that allows you to send an automated series of emails to prospects (that is, people who haven't yet moved through to the middle or bottom of your marketing funnel by donating, volunteering, etc.) in order to move them through your marketing funnel to a final action. In the for-profit world, prospects who aren't ready to buy, but who have expressed interest, are often referred to as "leads," which is where the name "lead nurturing" comes from. It's the same for your nonprofit. People who aren't ready to give, but are interested in your organization can be referred to as "leads" that must be nurtured.

While you may attract thousands of people to your organization's website every month, many of these visitors aren't ready to take the ultimate action of giving their time or money. People visit your website for various reasons that we've discussed in previous chapters. For this reason, it's important to provide calls-to-action that require top-of-the-funnel steps on the part of the prospect, such as, "subscribe to our blog or e-newsletter," "download a free report," "follow us on Facebook," etc., but also allow you to capture a minimal amount of contact information – a name and an email address. Once you have someone's email address, you can then begin the lead nurturing process – or in other words, building a relationship and trust – to move the person through your marketing funnel to eventually take a committed action to support your organization.

If you're sending your nurturing emails from an individual in your organization (an action that will result in higher open rates because the email is coming from a person versus the entire organization), make the first email in the series an introduction to that individual. List what types of content you'll be sharing over the next few weeks or months. Sending an introductory email helps set expectations and starts the conversation with your potential constituents.

**The benefits of lead nurturing**

Nurturing your top and middle-of-the-funnel prospects has numerous benefits. One, you significantly improve ROI. In the for-profit world, companies nurture their leads because it can cost hundreds of dollars per lead to get them. If they ignore these leads, they leave lots of money on the table – and these leads get scooped up and turned into customers by their competitors when they are ready to buy. It works the same for your nonprofit. You spend a lot time, money and effort to attract people to your website and/or organization; therefore, it pays to keep in contact with people versus ignoring them or thinking they're not valuable to you because they didn't take your most desired action right away.

Two, lead nurturing enables you to build thought leadership. Remember, we all do business with brands we know and trust. With lead nurturing, you build this trust by sending your prospects content that helps them get to know your organization a little better and see your organization's credibility through its impact.

Three, lead nurturing helps you to remain top-of-mind. According to the business-to-business research study, "Breaking Out of the Funnel," by Genius.com Incorporated, 70 percent of buyers indicated that "consistent and relevant communication was a key influencer in choosing a solution provider."

It works the same way for nonprofits. When people don't hear from your organization, they forget about you – fast. Can you remember what you had for dinner last week? Neither can we – so you can bet your prospects aren't going to remember an email blast you sent out a month ago. Targeted lead nurturing ensures people remember you because the content – and the action required – is geared toward your prospects and where they are in the giving cycle (which we discuss in just a bit).

And four, lead nurturing ties everything together. It begins to close the circle of your marketing efforts – moving people through the Methodology stages and the giving cycle from "strangers" to "advocates" – and sets your organization up to begin the last phase of the Inbound Marketing Methodology– inspiring people to become advocates for your cause.

**Lead nurturing = marketing love**

With a marketing automation tool, you can schedule emails to automatically go out whenever someone takes some sort of action on your website, and then send subsequent emails either hours, or days, after the first action is taken. Let's say, for example, someone subscribes to your blog or e-newsletter. You could simply send an automated welcome email. While a welcome email is important, it doesn't encourage your new subscriber to engage with your organization again and again. With marketing automation, you could send out another nurturing email – with a link to a piece of content – that helps you better qualify your prospect. You do this by having a link in the email go to a landing page with a form that may include a question the person has to answer that helps qualify him or her (Donor? Member? Volunteer?).

Lead nurturing also has one other huge benefit: timeliness. Study after study shows that email response rates decline over the age of the lead – meaning, the longer you wait to send an email after someone has given you his or her contact information, the less relevant your email becomes. In fact, in his Science of Timing research, Dan Zarrella, HubSpot's Inbound Marketing Scientist, discovered a positive correlation exists between subscriber recency and click-through rate (Figure 1), one of the key email engagement metrics. When you send an email as soon as, or within the hour, that a prospect takes an action on your website, you help move this person along your marketing funnel – at the precise time they've indicated they want to learn more about your organization.

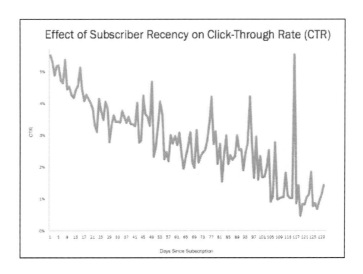

*Figure 1: The effect of subscriber recency on click-through rates*

## Sending the right content at the right time

So how exactly do you know which content to send to people and when? The first step is to understand your prospects' "giving cycle" – or other words, the steps they take when moving from strangers to donors, members, etc. This process typically has three stages: Awareness, Evaluation, and Action (Figure 2).

182

The Giving Cycle & supporting content:

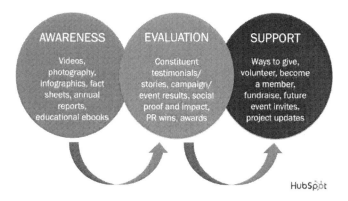

*Figure 2: The Giving Cycle and its supporting content*

In the Awareness stage, prospective constituents have become aware of your organization. In the Evaluation stage, your prospects know about your organization and that it might align with their need to become involved, donate, etc. In the Action stage, prospects do something: give, sign up, volunteer, etc. The giving cycle can happen in a matter of minutes – such as when someone comes to your organization's site and donates (think of how we give to the Red Cross during natural disasters) – or this process can take some time (days, weeks, months) as people learn more about your organization and how they can become involved.

Once you understand your giving cycle, you then use

Content Mapping to determine which content prospects receive depending on which phase of the giving cycle they're in. A person visiting your organization's website for the first time, for example, will have different informational requirements than someone who has already subscribed to your blog and has downloaded an annual report or visited your fundraising or "Get Involved" page. When developing content for each stage, think about how you can move people from "awareness" to "action" using relevant and useful content.

**Awareness stage**

At this stage, you'll want to begin with introductory, top-of-the-funnel content to help people become more familiar with your organization. Content such as blog posts, reports, and social media CTAs don't require much commitment from website visitors.

**Evaluation stage**

At this stage, people are evaluating your organization based on their own criteria and at their own pace. They also want to be sure your organization is one they can trust. Consider offering your annual report, volunteer stories and social proof that shows the impact your organization is having locally, nationally or globally. If it's important to your constituents, you may want to include "seals of approval" – e.g. an A+ rating from the Better Business Bureau or a rating from Charity Navigator. To reinforce social proof, consider mentioning awards and other recognitions that show your organization is one to be trusted.

## Action stage

Yay! Your hard work has paid off and now you've turned a prospect into a constituent. At this stage, you want to remain top of mind with them – and you want them to feel important and valued. In addition to sending a thank you email for whichever action they took, you may also want to consider sending invites or discounts to special "members only" or "donors only" events or other methods for making your constituents feel special. You can also encourage them to become a recurring donor, and suggest amounts they can give each month. Or, they can take their support to the field and volunteer to physically help your mission.

## Integrate lead nurturing with other inbound marketing tactics

To increase the efficiency and reach of your marketing campaigns, you'll want to integrate your landing pages with your lead nurturing, email marketing program, and social media. In fact, it's almost impossible to run effective lead nurturing campaigns in isolation of other marketing tactics as lead nurturing is so closely tied to them. To determine which content helps move people to become donors, members, etc., you'll want to track your landing page conversions by analyzing which offers compelled people to take specific actions. Using this information, you can then take your most successful content and either reuse it or repurpose it for your lead nurturing campaigns.

In addition to using landing pages and offers in your lead nurturing campaigns, you can also use your website pages and blog posts. Stories about or by constituents, success stories about the impact of donations, or reports "from the field" all make great content for lead nurturing campaigns – and help build trust in your organization, too. If you've created an email inviting your constituents to an event, or a timely campaign such as end of the year giving, you can repurpose this email and include it in your email nurturing campaigns for a period of time as well.

Integrating social media into your lead nurturing strategy also pays huge dividends. In fact, a GetResponse analysis reported that email newsletters with social sharing buttons had a 115 percent higher click-through rate than those that didn't. People want to share the content they enjoy reading, so as an inbound nonprofit, you'll want to make it easy for people to share your content by adding social buttons to your emails – both for sharing and for following. "Follow" buttons work differently from social share buttons as they enable email recipients to connect with your organization using one click. Including social follow buttons grows your reach and gives your prospects more touch points for interacting with your organization. The more points of contact a prospective constituent has with your organization, the more solidified your brand and message will be. Just be sure to make it clear what type of social buttons you're including, share versus follow.

**Measuring impact and closing the loop**

In order to understand the true impact of your lead nurturing campaigns, it's important that you measure your results as well as integrate closed-loop reporting. "Closing the loop" simply means that you analyze how people became "constituents" by understanding where they first came from and what content and/or actions took them through the giving cycle to make a commitment. By looking at the common patterns that brought in new constituents, you can then identify the behaviors you need to engage in to qualify future constituents and (gently) push them through your giving cycle more efficiently.

One important measurement is the cost to acquire constituents (CAC). To calculate this cost, take the amount you spent on marketing for a specific time period (usually done by month or quarter), including employee salary, and divide it by the number of new constituents for the same period: i.e. $10,000 /10 = $1,000 per constituent. This cost illustrates how much your organization is spending to acquire one new constituent. Your goal is to reduce this cost as much as possible while still growing your base. You can also break this out by persona (donors, volunteers, etc.). Knowing your CAC helps your team set realistic goals and budget how much your marketing department spends on which inbound tactics based on how many new constituents you need per month, quarter, or year.

Another way to measure the impact of your inbound marketing strategy is to calculate your Marketing Originated Constituent Percentage. Take all of the new constituents from a specific period and determine what percentage of them became constituents due to inbound marketing efforts. If 100 new people became constituents over the last 30 days and 50 came in due to your inbound marketing efforts, your Marketing Originated Constituent Percentage is: 100 / 50 = 50%. The higher this number, the better your impact using inbound marketing. It's good to take a baseline measurement about three months after you've implemented your new inbound marketing strategy. This way you have something against which to measure your growing impact.

Closed-loop reporting typically involves connecting your marketing analytics software with your customer relationship management (CRM) software. While this integration isn't necessarily complex, it is beyond the scope of this book. However, closed-loop marketing data is important as it helps you build your authority and supports your marketing decisions when reporting to your manager or your executive director and/or board members. Closed-loop reporting shows that your strategy is driven by results versus abstract theories or assumptions. It enables you to build powerful marketing presentations based on real data for board meetings, co-marketing partnerships, or writing grant proposals. For example, consider how much more impactful it would be to tell your manager or board that since you started blogging, you drove 45 percent more traffic to the organization's website, and of that traffic, you generated 15 new donors in 10 days – and your cost to acquire a new constituent has gone down to boot. What better way to both validate your inbound marketing efforts and show your worth!

If you want to learn more about closed-loop reporting, download, "An Introduction to Closed-Loop Reporting" at

**http://offers.hubspot.com/closed-loop-marketing**.

**To Do:**

1.  Write down if and how you nurture all your personas.

2.  Intermediate: Pick one persona you are not nurturing. Create a three email nurturing campaign that moves them through the giving cycle.

3.  _____

4.  _____

5.  _____

# Part Five

# **Inspire**

*"Donors don't give to institutions. They invest in ideas and people in whom they believe."*
**- G.T. Smith**

# Chapter 10
# **Empower your Inspired Advocates**

Up to this point, we've talked about how to move people through the marketing funnel – turning them from strangers into known constituents connected in some way to your organization. But, almost every organization has what we call Inspired Advocates – the individuals who give money repeatedly to your organization and volunteer for your events and campaigns. But more importantly, Inspired Advocates are the people who have shown they care about your mission and organization's future just as much as you do.

Because they care – passionately! – Inspired Advocates go above and beyond. They regularly share your content and stories, engage with you on social media, and forward your educational and informational emails to their networks. They even hold fundraising events and campaigns in their local communities. Because they're vocal – and often visible – it's important to keep Inspired Advocates in the forefront when building and executing your inbound marketing strategy. Your goal is to make these individuals feel really, really special. You want to take good care of them because they're the ones sending new strangers to your website – building awareness for your cause through their personal networks and in the process, giving your cause a "stamp of approval." In this chapter, you'll learn how to leverage the relationships you have with these individuals and how to empower them to become even more vocal about your cause.

**Create "Inspired Advocate" personas**

The interactions you have with Inspired Advocates are different from those of your regular constituent base. To ensure you correctly and continually identify these individuals – in order to create experiences and content tailored just for them – it helps to create "Inspired Advocate" personas for each of your constituent groups. When developing these personas, you'll want to determine: What motivates these individuals to become passionate advocates? What kinds of experiences do they want with our organization? How do they want to be thanked? What types of content do they want? What do they need from us in order to become even more vocal about our cause?

Depending on your type of organization and its size, you may have a couple dozen Inspired Advocates or a couple hundred. Spend some time tracking these individuals down and getting their contact information. Make sure everyone in your organization knows who these individuals are once you find them by talking about them, creating lists, and recognizing them whenever possible on your website, blog and on social media. You may even want to go as far as referring to them as "Inspired Advocate Martha" or "Inspired Advocate Sam" just so everyone internally knows you're referring to someone who is very special.

Once you've identified your Inspired Advocates and have created your persona, you can then develop an inbound marketing strategy that's tailored to leveraging the relationship Inspired Advocates have with your organization. To help them spread the word about your mission to even more people, consider the following easy tips.

**Develop content tailored specifically to them**

Inspired advocates no longer need to be moved through your marketing funnel, so instead of giving them the content your regular constituent base receives, create content tailored specifically for them to share. Take pictures from the field and share them with your advocates on Instagram or Facebook. Write blog posts that feature your advocates and their work. Create infographics that show the impact of donations – and ask your advocates to share them. Let them know your goals, how they can help you reach them and how their work has impacted your organization and the people it helps.

You can also use "smart content" on your website to ensure advocates see content tailored specifically to them. Using smart content and calls-to-action, the way Amazon does with their tailored suggestions, you can configure "rules" that allow you to show different content to your inspired advocates than what your regular constituent base sees. For example, if you have a free report that's behind a registration form, your regular constituent base sees the form. Using smart calls-to-action, your Inspired Advocates see only the "download now" button – they bypass the form altogether.

**Engage them on social media, consistently**

Another way to make your Inspired Advocates feel special, and keep them connected to your cause, is to engage them on social media on a consistent basis. In addition to regularly thanking them for sharing your content, you can do shout-outs of their work, retweet or repost their status updates and introduce them to other like-minded advocates. You also want to highly encourage them to share your stories, videos, and news with their networks. Leverage their voice to reach new audiences on any and all social networks on which have they have a presence.

**Keep in touch via email**

Another excellent strategy is to email your Inspired Advocates individually each quarter in order to gauge their advocacy and ask for their feedback. What types of events or campaigns do they have planned? What do they need from you to become even bigger advocates for your cause? Do they have any issues or concerns that need to be addressed – or feedback on how your organization can do something better or more efficiently?

One mistake you don't want to make is to send Inspired Advocates the same emails your regular constituent base receives – e.g. "join," "give," etc. Receiving these emails will make your Inspired Advocates feel like they're not special – and that you don't know who they are or how engaged they are with your mission. To ensure they receive emails tailored to them, exclude their names from your standard lists and create a list just for them.

**Give them free swag**

Inspired Advocates are worth their weight in gold. They've giving. They're volunteering. They're spreading the good word about your cause. They're fundraising on your behalf. One way to show you appreciate their efforts is to give them free swag (t-shirts, hats, water bottles, etc.) or even free VIP passes to events or free registration to upcoming events. You can also invite Inspired Advocates to a special luncheon or dinner with your board or Executive Director. Incentives are a great way to encourage Inspired Advocates to talk about you over and over again. And, who doesn't like free swag?

**Stay committed, have patience**

Becoming an Inbound Nonprofit does take time, patience and commitment – and, as we've shown you throughout this book, it happens one small step at a time. In order to get maximum value from your inbound marketing efforts in the form of more constituents, and ultimately, more donations, you need to give inbound marketing some effort – and faith. The benefits come slowly at first, but like a gym membership, the dedication and hard work pays off over time. The "secret" is to be consistent: stick to your blog editorial calendar, create content regularly that your constituents will want to download or share, and keep testing things to see what works.

You now have a framework for becoming an Inbound Nonprofit and growing your organization's visibility, reach and impact. We hope you've found the information in this book helpful and that it has inspired you to take action and get started – today. Inbound marketing has helped many organizations more than increase donations – it's helped them changed the world. We hope it changes yours, too.

**To Do:**

1. Identify if you have Inspired Advocates and create a new persona.

2. Follow your top ten major donors or most active fundraisers on Twitter.

3. Create one piece of content per month that is purely for these advocates to share. Highlight an achievement, tell a story or provide a campaign update.

4. _____

5. _____

# Glossary

**A/B Testing**

Testing two different versions of the same call-to-action or landing page in order to evaluate which one performs better.

**Above the fold**

The "fold" is an invisible line on your web page that separates a more desirable placement from a less desirable placement. "Above the fold" means people can see information without having to scroll. Search engines place some priority on content above the fold, since visitors see this content right away. It's generally a good practice to place your primary calls-to-action above the fold.

**Behavior-based marketing automation**

Behavior-based marketing automation refers to a system that triggers emails and other communication based on user activity on and off your site. Marketing automation enables marketers to nurture prospects and send them information only when it is most relevant to their giving cycle.

**Bitl.ly**

Bit.ly is a free URL shortening service that provides statistics for the links users share online. Bit.ly is used to condense long URLs to make them easier to share on social networks such as Twitter, Facebook, etc.

## Call-to-Action (CTA)

A call-to-action is a text link, button, image, or some type of web link that encourages a website visitor to visit a landing page and fill out a form. Some examples of CTAs are "Donate Now" or "Join Today."

## Campaign

An email marketing message or a series of messages, such as lead nurturing, designed to accomplish an overall marketing goal.

## Closed-loop marketing

Closed-loop marketing is marketing that relies on data and insights from closed-loop reporting. "Closing the loop" just means that sales teams report to Marketing about what happened to the leads that they received, which helps Marketing understand their best and worst lead sources.

## Closed-loop reporting

Campaign analytics that allow you to track precisely which of your marketing efforts are doing the best job of attracting the best types of customers to your website.

**CMS**

CMS is short for "content management system." A CMS is a software program that allows you to add content to a website more easily. HubSpot, for instance, has a CMS, through which you can manage your website pages, landing pages and blog.

**Content mapping**

The process for lead nurturing by which a marketing team prepares and organizes relevant and valuable content. Once organized, this content can be distributed to prospects depending on the type of lead and their point in the sales cycle.

**Conversion**

In the for-profit world, "conversion" is often defined in terms of sales, product or service inquiries. As a nonprofit, the conversion outcome is usually different: advocacy, volunteering, donating, fundraising.

**Conversion path**

The path that takes visitors from a targeted landing page to a contact form to the information or action they want. A defined conversion path prevents visitors from wandering around your website looking for the eBook, event, etc. that you promoted.

## CRM

Customer relationship management (CRM) is a system that manages interactions with existing and potential customers and sales prospects. Generally it's software that can either stand-alone or be incorporated with other software.

## CTR (Click-Through Rate)

CTR is the percentage (the number of unique clicks divided by the number that were opened) of recipients that click on a given URL in your email.

## Giving cycle

A process that consists of three steps, Awareness, Evaluation and Support that you use to help move people from "strangers" to constituents.

## Header

The top part of your blog, appearing before any pages or posts. Headers generally include items such as logos, taglines, and navigation menus, and are meant to set the tone or theme of your blog.

**Interruption-based marketing**

A traditional type of marketing in which audiences are interrupted with messages to purchase a product or a service. Interruption-based marketing is unsolicited and optimized for immediate conversions.

**Landing page**

A website page containing a form that revolves around a marketing offer, such as an eBook or a webinar, and serves to capture visitor information in exchange for the valuable offer.

**Lead**

A person that transforms from an anonymous website visitor into a known contact. This process occurs as the visitor provides his or her contact information in exchange for valuable content.

**Lead nurturing campaign**

Also known as email nurturing, lead nurturing refers to a series of emails triggered after someone fills out a form on a landing page.

**Meta tags**

Information found in a website's HTML code. Meta tags generally refer to a site's Title tags and meta description tags. Meta tags provide information about a given web page and help search engines categorize it correctly. Meta tags are not directly visible to people who visit a site.

**Offer**

The content that is provided once someone has filled out a landing page form. Examples of offers include eBooks, annual reports, webinars and kits.

**Persona**

More holistic and comprehensive than demographics, personas encompass the lifestyles, goals, challenges and aspirations of your constituents as well as personal and demographic information.

**PPC (Pay-per-Click)**

Advertising technique in which an advertiser puts an ad in an advertising venue, and pays that venue each time a visitor clicks on his/her ad. Google Adwords is the classic example of this.

**Privacy policy**

A clear description of a website or organization's policy on the use of information collected from and about website visitors and what they do, and do not do, with the data. Your privacy policy builds trust especially among those who opt-in to receive email from you or those who register on your site.

**Qualified lead (prospective constituent)**

A qualified lead, or prospective constituent, is a contact who opted in to receive communication from your organization and is interested in learning more.

**ROI**

Your marketing efforts "return on investment."

**RSS**

Short for Really Simple Syndication, a means by which users can subscribe to a feed, a blog feed, for instance. Since content is published on an ongoing basis, subscribing makes it easier for users to follow content and updates.

**Search Engine Optimization (SEO)**

Search engine optimization is the process of improving the volume

or quality of traffic to a website from search engines via unpaid or

organic search traffic.


**Segmentation**

Segmentation refers to the process of separating your target

audience into personas with different needs and preferences. These

segments will ideally be marketed to in a way that reflects their

specific experiences or interests.

**Social proof**

Social proof is the concept that people will conform to the actions of

others under the assumption that those actions are reflective of the

correct behavior. This third-party validation can be a very powerful

motivator for your site visitors' and prospects' actions.

**Reach**

The number of people listening to you. In social media, for example,

the more fans and followers you have for your social media

presence, the better reach you'll have. A larger reach translates into

a greater potential to generate more leads.

**Targeting**

Targeting encompasses sending emails to a select audience or group of individuals likely to be interested in the message. Targeting is very important for an email marketer because a relevant email campaign will yield a higher response rate and result in fewer unsubscribes.